G^{WITH}OD on a DEER HUNT

Steve Chapman

HARVEST HOUSE PUBLISHERS
EUGENE, OREGON 97402

Cover by Koechel Peterson & Associates, Minneapolis, Minnesota

WITH GOD ON A DEER HUNT
Copyright © 2001 by Steve Chapman
Published by Harvest House Publishers
Eugene, Oregon 97402

Library of Congress Cataloging-in-Publication Data
Chapman, Steve.
    With God on a deer hunt / Steve Chapman
        p. cm. — (Outdoor insights pocket devotional)
    ISBN 0-7369-0653-3
    1. Hunting—Religious aspects—Christianity. 2. Hunters—Prayer-books and
    devotions—English. I. Title. II. Series.
    BV4597.4.C43   2001
242'.68—dc21   2001016947

Printed in the United States of America

01 02 03 04 05 06 07 / BP-CF / 10 9 8 7 6 5 4 3 2 1

This book is dedicated to you.
It is my prayer that you
will be strengthened and encouraged
in your walk with God.

Acknowledgments

A very heartfelt thanks be to God who has given us the gift of His creation so we can learn about Him, our Maker.

A special thanks to Annie for sending me "out there!" The cookies are always good.

A word of appreciation to those who let me enjoy their property.

Thank you to Pastor Bill Rudd at Calvary Church in Fruitport, Michigan, for the insights that inspired "Twice Amazed" and "He Can, Can He?"

A note of thanks to John MacArthur for his commentary on the book of James that yielded the thoughts in "Look Intently."

Contents

A Note from Steve

"Since the creation of the world His invisible attributes, His eternal power and divine nature, have been clearly seen, being understood through what has been made, so that they are without excuse." These inspiring words from Romans 1:20 express an undeniable truth: The outdoors is one of the best places to improve the "inner man." If we take the time to "get out there," God will make Himself known in ways we never expected.

For those who do go outside (as well as for those who can't), *With God on a Deer Hunt* is a guide to some of the riches available in the woods. May you use these pages as a springboard to other outdoor insights God will show you if you ask Him to.

1

Jackson's Wait

*This is the day which the LORD has made;
let us rejoice and be glad in it.*

Psalm 118:24

Jackson is an inquisitive, five-year-old neighbor boy who showed up one summer day in my backyard as I was preparing to practice with my compound bow. "What ya doin'?" was the first of a thousand questions.

As I removed my bow and arrows from the case, his eyes widened. I instructed him to stand safely behind me as I took a few shots. Stride for stride he followed me back and forth as I shot and retrieved my arrows. The conversation was endless. And this would not be the last time I would have company as I practiced that summer. I suspected that the seeds sown during our time together might someday yield a full-grown hunter.

Finally deer season arrived and, as I had promised Jackson, I managed to deliver a load of venison to his family. As I stood in their kitchen describing the hunt, Jackson was listening. The look on his face revealed a youthful hunger to go into the woods that demanded a response.

"Jackson, would you and your dad like to sit in a ground blind with me next week?"

He nearly passed out with excitement as he looked at his parents with that "Oh! Please don't say no!" look. They didn't refuse him, so we set a date and I went home. Little did I know what a dilemma I had created for their entire family. For days Jackson woke up and went to bed asking, "How much longer till I go hunting?" His dad described the torture to me later, and we had some chuckles over it. (At least I did.)

Having raised two children, I suppose I should have known better than ask him so early. However, time had erased the memory of what kids are like when they are intensely anticipating an event. Time creeps too slowly. Hours are weeks, and days are months. Jackson's inability to wait patiently wore heavily on the nerves of everyone around him. I even got a taste of it whenever he showed up under our second floor patio: "We still goin' huntin', Mr. Chapman?" He was relentless. He could be comforted only by one answer: "Sure are, little buddy!"

As grueling as the wait might have been for my young neighbor (and his family), there was something beautiful about it. Romans 8:19 states that creation itself "waits eagerly for the revealing of the sons of God." Because of the distortion that sin brought into humanity's relationship with God, the earth "groans" (not a complaining sound, but a sigh at the reality of living in a sinful world) for redemption. It longs to know the uncorrupted presence of those whose spirits belong to a holy God.

The day will come when all of creation—including our aching, aging bodies—will be set free from the slavery of deterioration. Until it comes to pass, there is only one hope that can comfort our anxious hearts. It is knowing that our spirits have already been redeemed as a result of another day that was eagerly anticipated—"when the kindness of God our Savior and His love for mankind appeared, He saved us" (Titus 3:4,5). That was the greatest day the Lord ever made!

Oh, my blessed Redeemer, blessed be the day You appeared with salvation for the sons and daughters of man. As I sit in the midst of creation and contemplate its longing for redemption, I rejoice that I am already Your own. With an anticipation that rivals that of an excited child, I am waiting for You to come and restore this earth to Your glory. In Jesus, my Deliverer's name, I pray, amen.

2

Life in the Leaf

*He will be like a tree firmly planted
by streams of water, which yields its fruit
in its season and its leaf does not wither.*

Psalm 1:3

When deer hunting season returns, summer is behind us and the foreboding winter lies ahead. It is autumn, a time when something sober begins to happen to the leaves that have been alive since the spring. A certain dry curl at their edges silently speaks of their impending demise. Though still mostly green at the end of September, the life source is slowly being drawn from them. There is no way to stop the process.

I am 50 years old now. It feels like my "autumn" has arrived. There's a peculiar dryness about my joints that is troublesome. Other body parts are showing the effects of the years, especially my hairline. Bones that didn't ache before are speaking to me. As far as my eyes are concerned, forget the longer arms idea—pass me my glasses! I feel like my friend who turned 50 a few weeks before me. When I asked him how it felt, he responded, "Hey! I feel like a teenager..." He paused for a moment then added with a tired sigh, "...that's been in a wreck!"

Thankfully, though the body is undeniably decaying, Psalm 1 offers every human the hope of being like a tree with eternal foliage. But there are prerequisites. They are found in the first two verses of the chapter: "How blessed is the man who does not walk in the counsel of the wicked, nor stand in the path of sinners, nor sit in the seat of scoffers! But his delight is in the law of the LORD, and in His law he meditates day and night."

I want to be that man—bold enough to avoid the pitfall of listening to the lies of those who do not embrace the wisdom of the Lord. I want to walk close to my Creator and not stand where sinners tread back and forth to their wickedness. For that reason, today I will take advantage of the quietness of the deer stand to ponder the mandates and the ways of my God. As I search the woods with my eyes, I will scan the Scriptures stored in my heart and meditate on God's truth. In them, my "leaves" will find life.

Lord, thank You for the privilege of coming into Your presence. As I bring Your truth to my remembrance, teach me in these quiet moments so that my life's roots can burrow even deeper into the security of knowing You. In Jesus, my Lifegiver's name, I pray, amen.

3

The Slap

Arise, O LORD; save me, O my God!
For You have smitten all my enemies on the cheek;
You have shattered the teeth of the wicked.

Psalm 3:7

Not too many hunts ago, I was sitting quietly in my tree-stand growing more angry by the minute at the mosquitoes that were driving me insane. One of the pesky bugs landed on my face and started boring into my upper jaw. Disregarding the risk of too much motion or noise, I slapped the stupid thing and mashed it before it deposited too much venom. Unfortunately, I also managed to seriously rattle my own cage. As I was recovering from the self-inflicted blow to my poor head, I thought of the story my wife, Annie, tells about the day she silenced an enemy.

The younger, obnoxious brother of an older, nasty-minded fellow mercilessly teased her during a morning bus ride to high school. It was not the first time he tortured her with comments that falsely accused her of being attracted to his deviant elder brother. It was humiliating and embarrassing, and it continued as the bus rolled down the highway. However, the siege against Annie's crumbling emotions soon came to an abrupt end. She had had enough.

Annie faced her accuser in his seat and stared squarely into his eyes. Then, without any consideration for her safety or reputation, she drew back her right arm as far as she could and released the string on an unbelievably forceful slap across the face of her nemesis.

On impact, she claims, the boy's eyes that were crossed became uncrossed for a brief moment. The sound of the hand-on-cheek explosion was deafening. The sudden noise of teeth banging violently against one another was excruciating to hear. The deed was done. Only the low roar of the heavy tires on pavement filled the bus until it arrived at school.

That happened more than 30 years ago and to this day, somewhere in the hills of West Virginia, the echo of that slap is still bouncing through time. The outcome? Never again was Annie teased by the young snit whose lights were so significantly dimmed, even if only momentarily. Though she readily admits her retaliation was not the most appropriate way to handle the situation, I'm proud of my wife for her courage. (And I try to never make her mad!)

Annie's slap on the jaw of the kid that provoked her is a vivid picture of today's verse. Some of us may have enemies who are spreading rumors about us or adversaries determined to undermine our businesses. Some may even have foes who want to do bodily harm. Isn't it great that we can say, "Blessed is the one who comes to the defense of our souls and shuts up our accusers!" And we can praise God for the outcome of His deliverance: "Salvation belongs to the LORD; Your blessing be upon Your people!" (Psalm 3:8).

Lord, thank You for hearing my spirit's cries for help. Your hand is mighty and able to deliver. Only You can silence my enemies. Please come to my defense; my deliverance belongs to You. You alone are the shield for my soul and the lifter of my head in the face of my accusers. In the blessed name of Christ I pray, amen.

4

The Farmer
and the Field

*The seed in the good soil, these are the ones who have
heard the word in an honest and good heart, and hold it
fast, and bear fruit with perseverance.*

Luke 8:15

The trails were well used but the ground around them
was unmarked by bedding depressions and droppings.
The deer were passing through but not stopping on my
little piece of property. I decided a food plot might entice
them to linger for a while and with good deerstand place-
ment, my few acres could hold some promise for a suc-
cessful hunt come October.

I picked out an area along a creek bed and cleared
some timber so the sunlight would reach the ground.
Before hauling a heavy, gas-powered tiller into the remote
spot, I tested the soil with my three-pound mattock.
When I lifted the heavy tool over my head and brought it
down into the dirt I struck rock. My teeth rattled and my
vision blurred upon impact. Everywhere I dropped the
mattock I heard the telltale steel-on-stone sound. I knew
the job would be bigger than I had planned.

For the next several days it was dig and throw, dig and
throw. I guess I tossed at least 1,000 softball-sized stones
into the creek. And the various roots I had to dig up were
long and tangled. It was an exhausting process. On the
third day of preparing the ground, I thought of the
chorus of a song I had written several years before when

my children were much younger. It is titled "The Farmer and the Field" and it goes like this:

> He was the farmer, I was the field
> And it always hurt when the ground was tilled
> But he was getting rid of the rocks and the weeds
> So the ground would be good when he sowed the seed.

The lyrics are the words of a wise son spoken in honor of an earthly father who was diligent to discipline him when he had done wrong. The dad was careful to do so because he understood that only "good soil" is able to successfully receive the imperishable seed of the Word of God. He was aware that the ground of the human heart is made good only through the hauling away of the rocks and weeds that would choke the seed. The son's wise father also knew another important element of being a parent/farmer: Compassion must accompany correction. While my rocky food-plot-to-be may not feel the forceful blows of my weighty mattock, the human heart does not escape the pain. The son's compliments to his dad indicated that the father had done well.

What was the result? Like my now green-and-delicious quarter of an acre, the dad harvested a son whose life displayed the fruit of the eternal seed of the Scriptures. Taking the time to prepare the soil of a child's heart is worth the effort!

Lord, thank You for being my kind Father. And thank You for the children You have given me. Please help me be diligent to discipline. I pray for Your mercy and compassion to flow through me as I prepare their hearts for Your good seed. And on that day when I finally see the fruit of my labor, I'll give You the glory. In Jesus' name I pray, amen.

5

Don't Give In

Do not give the devil an opportunity.

Ephesians 4:27

One of the places I'm privileged to hunt is about 60 miles from my house. Occasionally, as I start up the entrance ramp to the highway, I think of a story I once heard:

> An old southern farmer who looked and sounded like "Mr. Haney" on the classic TV show "Green Acres," was in his rattletrap truck approaching the entrance to a busy, city freeway. As he puttered onto the four-lane, a well-dressed businessman barreling down the road in his fancy, late-model sports car suddenly slammed into him. The two men exited their wrecked vehicles. The raging city slicker stomped over to the farmer.
>
> "Hey, you crazy hick! Didn't you see the yield sign?"
>
> The farmer removed his dirty hat, scratched his head as he surveyed the damage to his truck, and replied with an indignant country drawl, "I *yield* at ya three times, mister, and ya wouldn't git over!"

Now there's a man who had set his course and was not about to be deterred. Though his simpleminded oversight of the laws of the highway cannot be defended, the seasoned country gentleman has to be admired for his unwavering determination.

When it comes to the enticements that the enemy of my soul offers, I want to be like that old farmer. I want to ignore the yield signs. The opportunity to make a decision like this came one day several years ago when a man challenged my attitude about maintaining social exclusivity with my wife. He thought my stance about never being alone with another woman in a public or private setting was archaic and prudish. His suggestion was to "branch out, be a free spirit." Without hesitation I dismissed his advice as misleading and dangerous. His counsel reminded me of Colossians 2:8: "See to it that no one takes you captive through philosophy and empty deception, according to the tradition of men, according to the elementary principles of the world, rather than according to Christ." Another passage warns, "If sinners entice you, do not consent" (Proverbs 1:10). And still another says, "The wisdom of this world is foolishness before God" (1 Corinthians 3:19). Not too many months after the man offered his poisonous opinion, I learned he had been caught in an adulterous affair and was eventually served with divorce papers. I felt sorry for him, but I did feel justified in not yielding my position.

Perhaps the next time you venture onto a freeway and see one of those triangle-shaped signs that say "Yield," you'll remember the old farmer and think of the words of wisdom: "Do not give the devil an opportunity."

Father, I bring to You a heart of gratitude for the strength You provide to help me say a firm no to the enemy of my soul. Whatever the cost, may all the roads of relationships and pursuits that I enter find me unyielding to any bad advice and misdirection the world may offer. In Jesus' name I pray, amen.

6

The Grunt Call

My sheep hear My voice,
and I know them, and they follow Me.
John 10:27

It was a red-letter day for me when, for the first time, a buck responded to my grunt call. I'll never forget how he suddenly appeared about 45 yards in front of my tree-stand. He was walking in the openness of a logging road. Instead of leaving it and coming toward me on the trail that passed near my stand, he continued moving from my left to right at too far a distance for my arrow.

Because my nerves tend to turn into a bowl of shaky Jello when a deer appears, I almost forgot about the grunt call that was hanging on the lanyard around my neck. When I finally remembered it was there, it was nearly too late. As the deer stepped into the woods on the other side of the road and began to head away from my position, I quickly scrambled to get the call to my mouth.

When I pushed the air through the tube the sound it made was meant to say, "Hey! I'm one of you! Over here. Stop. Come back!"

At the familiar sound of the call, the buck halted in his tracks and looked directly toward my stand. His uncanny ability to key in on my location was amazing. He stood for a few seconds, showed only a slight interest in what he had heard, then turned and once again started walking away.

I sent a second, gentler blast of air through the call.

Once more he stopped and looked my way. His pause was slightly longer, but he seemed determined to continue in the opposite direction. When he turned yet again to leave I blew once more. This time my heart nearly jumped out of my shirt when he wheeled around on his back hooves and started toward my stand. I carefully lowered the call to my chest, attached my release to the string, and prepared for the shot. I was already standing and by the time I came to full draw the buck was about 12 yards from my tree. The rest of the story is wrapped up and stored safely in my freezer.

I was absolutely amazed that I, a human, could connect vocally with such an animal as the elusive whitetail deer. Using a manmade device I had actually spoken to a creature that is not just different from me in degree, but in kind. He and I had nothing in common except that we both occupied space on the planet. The deer would not someday evolve into a man, nor would I, through many reincarnations, return someday as a whitetail. Yet I "spoke" to that deer and he answered. Incredible!

As I pondered the extraordinary fact that I had managed to communicate with the buck, I thought of how amazing it is that God can speak to people. We are also vastly different in kind. Yet God fully knows how to bridge the gap between Himself and humans. It is astounding to realize we can actually hear Him speak.

In John 10, a beautiful analogy is given regarding God's relationship to mankind. Those who follow Him are referred to as His sheep and God is called the Good Shepherd. In verse four it is a written that four-legged sheep follow their master because they know his voice. "A stranger they simply will not follow, but will flee from him, because they do not know the voice..." (verse 5).

This physical picture of a spiritual reality shows the marvelous truth that mankind is able to "key in" on God's call to his heart.

When do we hear Him? Romans 8:16 points out, "The Spirit Himself bears witness with our spirit that we are children of God." You may be wondering if you have ever heard His voice. Was there ever a time when you were headed down the road of sin and had turned away from God in disobedience? Somewhere deep inside your heart did you hear, "Don't go that way. It is wrong! Turn around!" At that moment, did you stop and look to the Lord? If so, you heard the voice of the Good Shepherd. He who is eternal connected with you in that moment. And if you turned back toward Him, you were divinely enticed like a buck to a grunt call.

Unlike deer hunters who use our artificial calls to draw in a deer to *take* its life, Jesus calls us to Himself so that He can *give* us everlasting life. That, my friend, is the Good News! Have you responded to His call?

My God and the keeper of my soul, thank You that You call out to the hearts of people. I pray to always hear You when You speak. I ask for discernment to know when it is not Your voice. Help me always come Your way when You call. In Jesus' name, amen.

7

The Markings

I am fearfully and wonderfully made.

Psalm 139:14

Back in the 70s, my uncle, David Chapman, purchased a 30-30 caliber rifle. During a visit with him last year, he offered to sell it to me. Without hesitation I took him up on it. Why? Because the gun was not just a standard issue rifle. There was a special inscription on the barrel that read, "Winchester–Model 94/NRA Centennial Model/ 1871–1971." The gun had never been fired, and it was in mint condition. I thought about shooting a few rounds through it just to say I was the first to feel its smooth kick; however, I decided to keep it in its most valuable state. It is now safely stored and gaining daily in value as it ages toward antiquity in its protective case.

Perhaps someday in the distant future someone might even end up appearing with it on one of my wife's favorite TV programs, the "Antiques Roadshow," which features appraisals of items of age and uniqueness. On occasion, viewers get to see some interesting looks on the faces of those who present their treasures. Annie loves it when they gasp in pleasant surprise that the thing they thought was worth only a few dollars turns out to be appraised for a figure that exceeds a five-year total of their annual income.

For example, one lady took a lamp to the show that had hideous lizards formed in stained glass on its shade. I fully agreed with Annie's reaction when she saw it: "I wouldn't put that thing in my house if you paid me. How ugly!" Then the appraiser turned the lamp over and there it was: *Tiffanys of New York!* Suddenly the lackluster lamp became an item worth fighting for. Annie's next response was, "Well…just maybe I could find a place for it somewhere in the house."

How a piece is marked makes all the difference. It's true for antiques and it's certainly true for humans. Other people might look at us and see only our unsightly features. Physical imperfections, limited abilities, a past that haunts us, lack of wealth, and other flaws that are unattractive might justify their negative appraisal of us. However, if they look under the surface and into our hearts they will find that distinguishing mark that makes onlookers sit up and take notice. They are the words written in Psalm 139:14: "fearfully and wonderfully made."

What we look like, what we have or don't have, and what others think of us do not determine our value. Instead, it's the mark of the God who made us that gives us distinct and ultimate worth. With that in mind, may we be careful to look at ourselves as well as those around us not according to the outward, fleshly appearance but in regard to the spirit of God that dwells inside.

Dear Lord, I thank You that I am fearfully and wonderfully made. Please help me remember this comforting truth when I am tempted to appraise my worth by the standards of the world. Help me recognize those around me the way You see them—priceless by design. In Jesus' name, amen.

8

Look Intently

*But one who looks intently at the perfect law,
the law of liberty, and abides by it, not having become a
forgetful hearer but an effectual doer,
this man will be blessed in what he does.*

James 1:25

Whitetail hunters who spend enough time in the woods where there is plenty of good cover for the animals sooner or later encounter a most intriguing phenomenon. Even though the foliage may be dense, there are times when a deer can slip within a few yards of a person and stand there totally undetected. Portions of their motionless form might show, but the hunter may never see it. Not knowing it is there, he could decide to scratch his nose— and the discernible gesture will likely send the wary critter scampering away!

I have had times when I was scanning the woods looking for movement when suddenly a spot in the brush that was light and open a few moments before is now dark and closed. I have visually gone on by it and continued my radarlike search. Then, as if the information is on a five-second delay, a bell in my brain goes off. My eyes return to the spot, and I peer at it for more than a little while. Then, lo and behold, there's an eye with that familiar, pale-white circle around it staring through the opening. As I study it closer and follow the lines, I see the tip of an ear. Upon closer examination of the immediate area below the ear and eye, I see sticks that amazingly turn into fur-covered legs.

At that point my heart rate soars, and I have to control my breathing and fight the urge to quickly raise my bow or gun. Oh! How I love it when that vague shape suddenly transforms into a deer. Knowing that I have been astute enough to take the necessary time to look closely and not miss the details is a most rewarding feeling. It's one of those things that keeps me going back to the woods year after year.

The way that a close inspection of heavy foliage often reveals a well-hidden deer and gets a hunter's pulse to rise is the same way a close look at the Scriptures can expose truth and inspire the reader. In today's passage, the words "looks intently" have a stronger meaning than you may realize. In the original language, it refers to stooping over and carefully peering at something from all possible vantage points. It's the way Peter looked into the empty tomb; he gave it a very thorough examination. Someone who looks into the Scriptures in this way will not only discover life-altering truths, but he will be so moved by them that a change of heart occurs. The individual becomes not just a reader, but a doer of the Word.

One who looks at the Word of God and goes on unchanged is described as a person who looks at himself in a mirror, turns away, and immediately forgets what kind of person he is. While he may have clearly seen his own image, he is either quickly distracted or uninterested. Tragically, the benefits of the Word of God in this person's life is lost. (See verses 23,24.)

It's impossible to know how many deer I have never seen because I didn't make the effort to really study the woods. And when it comes to the Scriptures, I shudder to think what I have missed as a result of reading it with no particular motivation other than curiosity or just "getting in a daily quota." I want to do better. I have a feeling you do, too.

Thank You, Lord, for Your Word. It is filled with the truth about Your marvelous love and amazing ability to save us. Help me not only see deeper into Your Word, but also to be a doer of what You reveal. May none of Your truths be lost to casual eyes. I ask for Your strength and patience to look intently at Your sayings. In Jesus' name, amen.

The Oxygen Mask

Then I will teach transgressors Your ways,
and sinners will be converted to You.

Psalm 51:13

I suppose it seems strange that I enjoy climbing into the heights of a treestand to hunt but truly dislike flying in airplanes. The truth is, the actual ascent doesn't bother me, it's the steady flying that leaves me tired and tense. Though it saves time and wear and tear on my body, my emotions take a beating when I fly. I'm one of those people who returns a look of terror when someone asks, "What's your *final* destination?" (I wish they wouldn't use that word!) And when a person asks, "Do you have reservations?" my standard response is a nervous, "Should I? Is there something wrong with the plane? Of course I have reservations! I don't want to get on it!"

Because of my ongoing resistance to being a projectile wildly hurled through the skies at breakneck speeds, I am always attentive to the safety speech the flight attendants give before takeoff. While others read their newspapers or talk to their neighbors, my eyes are usually focused on the front of the cabin. On one particular flight, as the lady attendant was delivering her safety sermon, a certain word caught my ear. I had just read a Scripture that used it. The word was "then." She used it this way:

In the unlikely event of a loss of cabin pressure, a panel will open above you and a mask will fall down. Reach up, take the mask, place it over your nose and mouth, adjust the tabs, and breathe normally. [Right!] If you have a child with you, put the mask on yourself first, *then* assist your child.

In Psalm 51, David's cry for God's cleansing after he sinned with Bathsheba is recorded. He begs, "Wash me thoroughly from my iniquity and cleanse me from my sin....Wash me, and I shall be whiter than snow.... And blot out all my iniquities. Create in me a clean heart, O God, and renew a steadfast spirit within me. Do not cast me away from Your presence" (Psalm 51:2,7,9-11). Finally, verse 13 begins with the particular word that caught my ear: "*Then* I will teach transgressors Your ways." (Though *then* is not in the original language, it is appropriately included.)

That day on the airplane a life-changing thought occurred to me. When the flight attendant gave the instructions regarding the masks and children, her discourse was more profound than she might have realized. In it was a picture of the order we are to follow if we care about the spiritual well-being of our children. In a world that is in trouble and morally spiraling out of control, parents must be the first to take in the life-giving breath of Christ. There is no way we can effectively assist our kids if we are spiritually unconscious. We need to let God cleanse our hearts from our sins and cause us to have willing spirits to let Him do it daily. It is crucial that we lean on Him for purification so we can better teach our "little transgressors" His ways.

Dear Lord, thank You for allowing me this time in Your presence. Forgive me for my offenses to You. It is against You, and You alone, that I have sinned. Cleanse and renew me. As a parent, I seek the joy of Your forgiveness so that I, in turn, can lead my children to know it as well. You teach that it is the "prayers of a righteous man that accomplishes much." Help me, by Your grace, to be a pursuer of holiness. Without it, I am unable and unqualified to lead my children to the life-giving breath You want to breathe into their lives. In Your name I pray, amen.

10

In the Spotlight

Many are saying, "Who will show us any good?"
Lift up the light of Your countenance upon us, O LORD.
Psalm 4:6

I suspect nearly all of us have inadvertently spotlighted deer with our headlights. Those green, glowing eyes in the high beams are an immediate giveaway of an animal's presence. It is always a delight to behold such an illusive creature, even in the artificial ray of manmade sunshine.

I wonder how it feels to be spotlighted. Do the deer ask, "What possible thrill can those humans get out of blinding us this way?" I suppose they don't think anything of it because, if left unapproached, they seem to just go on about their business, enjoying their meal and standing around.

Though I have never been lit up in an open field by the glare of a powerful electric torch, I do belong to a "herd" that has been spotlighted. Psalm 4:6, today's verse, unreservedly illuminates those who belong to God. I find it sobering that the Lord, with all the natural beauty of His universe available to be displayed, would choose to draw the attention of a seeking world to His people. Perhaps He does so because those who long to see something good are wondering if it really is possible, for example, to be deeply glad. They question if anyone can find more happiness than what is produced by their mind-numbing alcohol or drugs. They wonder if it is remotely possible to find true rest when they put their heads on their pillows at night. They doubt that on all of the planet there is a refuge from the constant threat of danger.

These are desires that humans crave. And, rightly so, the best evidence that God is their source for human wishes will be found in others who are experiencing them. For that reason, we who gather with God in His field of provision are going to get the spotlight. The good news is that our job is to go on with what we are enjoying in Him. Like the deer in the field, we don't have to act differently. Just be what we are…partakers of God's goodness. Those who see us will be drawn to our contentment and sense of safety. As they look longingly into our field, may we be careful to invite them in. There's plenty of provision for everyone!

Thank You, Father, for Your bountiful love toward us. I am aware that many in this world desperately hope to see something that yields evidence that Your goodness exists. Some of these people live in ghetto filth, some in war-torn towns. Others live in nice houses in clean neighborhoods where the walls sometimes conceal terrors such as abuse and emotional woundings. Whoever they are, if their eyes turn to me, may they see only the result of a heart that has found delight in You. Make my joy complete. As the peace You give fills me, may it reflect only You when the light shines on me. In Jesus' name, amen.

11

When God
Goes Hunting

He has bent His bow and made it ready.
Psalm 7:12

I've tried to imagine what a deer feels when it suddenly realizes that someone or something is pursuing it. The way its tail flares up and its body crouches in readiness to spring into an escape makes me wonder if it is not only responding to an instinct to survive, but if there is a humanlike fear that grips its mind. Whatever the case may be, deer obviously react to being hunted.

When do humans feel the intense fear of being pursued? Soldiers have certainly felt it. Those who have encountered the evil intentions of a criminal have dealt with it. And some of us have unexpectedly become the hunted when we've faced, for example, the unhappy attitude of a mother bear protecting her cub. While these situations may give way to an adrenaline-drenched terror, there is a time far more serious that generates the absolute worst of emotions. It is when God goes hunting after an unrepentant heart.

The words of Psalm 7:12,13 would be frightening to read if someone were refusing to yield to God: "If a man does not repent, [God] will sharpen His sword; He has bent His bow and made it ready. He has also prepared for Himself deadly weapons; He makes His arrows fiery shafts." The sobering thought about God's ability to stalk a stubborn soul is that He will surely find it. Realizing this, the only way to avoid His flaming arrows or His finely sharpened sword is to submit in repentance.

The amazing truth is that while "it is a terrifying thing to fall into the hands of the living God," there is a strange comfort in understanding why He comes after us when we balk at repentance. God hunts us because He loves us enough to capture us!

Before God ever nocks an arrow or uses His whetstone to sharpen His sword, it would be wise to kneel on the knees of the heart and submit in repentance. Otherwise, go hide…if you think you can!

O Lord, I know there have been times I would not repent. Yet You came after me because You love me. Thank You! From now on I want to remember that when I fail by sinning against You, running away would be a mistake because You are too good a hunter! Blessed be Your name. Amen.

12

The Drive-Through

Come to Me, all who are weary and
heavy-laden, and I will give you rest.
Matthew 11:28

One of the greatest by-products of hunting from a deer stand is sitting still. Even if only for an hour or two, deer hunting can seem like a vacation to a tired soul. One muscle, especially for me, that needs to rest is my brain. My overactive mind can tire me out as quickly as any other part of my body. Far too many nights of sleep have ended prematurely because my mind woke up before my body was ready.

Perhaps you can relate to this embarrassing, but true, story and agree that it is very important to occasionally give the brain a break.

One morning I drove to a town 25 miles from home to take care of some business. I was anxious to get it done so I would have an opportunity to hunt that afternoon. I skipped breakfast at the house and by midmorning I was feeling hunger pangs. Even though I didn't have a minute to spare, I pulled into a fast-food drive-through and placed an order. I was given the total and instructed to pull to the first window. I paid for my food and received about 90 cents in change. I was then directed to the second window.

As I sat at the opening, I could see inside the restaurant. I watched the employees as they slowly lumbered around, talked to each other, laughed, and generally had a merry old time—at the expense of my schedule! I found myself beginning to steam at the sight. I nervously fidgeted with the change I held in the palm of my hand. The swarm of thoughts of all I had yet to do while in town (and all I wanted to say to the manager of the restaurant) began to distort my intelligence. Suddenly, the handful of coins I was palming turned into a payment yet to be made. I thought, *Since I haven't paid and they don't have my money, they're not gonna get any more of my time!* At that, I promptly drove away. I was about two miles down the road before it hit me. My countenance went from a look of mischief to horrible embarrassment. Did I go back? No way! I wasn't about to show my stupid face to that bunch. I fought the hunger. I will admit that a satisfying feeling washed over me when I realized that behind me was a drive-through in total chaos. I could almost hear the window attendant screaming in confusion as angry customers kept saying, "Hey! You numbskull. This is not my order!" I hate to admit it, but I hoped the mix-ups went on for hours.

To say the least, the evening hunt was good therapy for my frazzled brain. I was the better for it. To sit for a while and rest was just what the doctor ordered.

The spirit can gain much benefit from a mind that can find calm. Those who have emotionally worked to exhaustion, who find themselves sitting frustrated in the drive-throughs of life, desperately need a place to retreat. Where can our spirits go to find rest? While a quiet treestand might be a good place for a tired body, it is not the true place of solace for the spirit. Keep in mind that only if the heart leans for a while on the presence of Christ will you find the ultimate comfort. Remember the wisdom of Isaiah 26:3 (NKJV): "You will keep him in perfect peace, whose mind is stayed on You." May today's quiet vigil in your stand be more than just a deer hunt. May it be a time when you can be still and know God.

Dear Lord, I need true rest—not just for my body but for my spirit as well. Thank You for this time You have given me to be quiet. I'm grateful that I can be here with You. Help me to be still and know You are God. In Jesus' name, so be it.

13

The Watch

I will seek the lost, bring back the scattered,
bind up the broken and strengthen the sick.
Ezekiel 34:16

It only took one episode of leaving home for a hunt without a wristwatch to teach me a good lesson. I managed to miss an important meeting because I didn't head back on time. For that reason, I mounted a used Timex to my bow. I cut the straps off and taped the timepiece to the inside of the riser. From then on, I haven't made the mistake of misjudging time.

As I was cutting the band of the perfectly good watch, I thought about what my dad had done years earlier at our church youth camp. He had been invited to speak to the youths who had gathered for a week, and his illustration was brilliant. It was so moving, in fact, that it is still with me today.

Without any of us knowing it, when Dad arrived at the camp he stashed a brick, a hammer, and a screwdriver in the pulpit. In his pocket was a beautiful, colorful wristwatch. When he was introduced, the first thing he did was pull the watch out of his coat and ask who would like to have it. Every hand waved vigorously. Dad picked a young man and asked him to come forward. As he put out his hand to take the watch, Dad pulled it back and said, "Just a second. Before I give this to you, I want to do something to it."

At that, Dad took out the items he had hidden. He proceeded to lay the watch on the hard brick, place the screwdriver blade in the center of the crystal, and, with a powerful blow of the hammer, hit the top of the screwdriver handle. Watch parts flew all over the room! Quickly he gathered up as much as he could find and piled it into the boy's open hand. Absolute shock was evident in the young fellow's face as he returned to his seat with the worthless remains of what used to be a gorgeous timepiece. The rest of us sat in stunned silence as Dad taught us about the sad mistake of unnecessarily destroying our lives before we give them over to Christ.

Knowing that some of us had already done self-damage, my dad ended his illustration with the hope we all needed: "There's no way I can rebuild the watch my young friend has in his hands; however, God is able to reconstruct our lives. He even knows where all the parts are. None of them is lost to Him. He wants to gather them up and restore us to the beauty and usefulness we once held. Do you want Him to do it?"

The altar area filled with young people and tears flowed.

Dad's unforgettable illustration might be what you needed to hear today. If you're wearing a watch, take a look at it. Now is the time to let God begin His repairs. He can make you useful again.

Father in heaven, thank You that I can bring my broken life to You. Sin has scattered me beyond self-repair. Please take the remnants I offer and make me useful again. My time is in Your hands. In Christ's name, amen.

14

A Select Arrow

He has also made Me a select arrow,
He has hidden Me in His quiver.
Isaiah 49:2

While archery deer season might have its legal limits in terms of the calendar, it lasts 365 days a year for me. This is true because during the off-season I am always tweaking my equipment, trying to improve my advantage against the elusive whitetail. One of the things I enjoy working on is culling my inventory of arrows, keeping only the best for the moment of truth, even though the opportunity may still be months away.

When the season finally arrives, after settling into a deerstand, it is without exception a special moment for me when I remove an arrow from my quiver. Knowing that a second shot might be hard to come by, I am careful to pick an arrow that has a certain mark I have inscribed on its plastic vane: #1. It wears that title because it has been tested and proved it was dependable. To use it is a boost to my confidence level. More importantly, if all goes well in the aiming process, the animal will suffer far less.

I try to fill my quiver with #1s. To go into the woods with less than the best is risky. As a result, there's a strange bond between me and my "aluminum friends." Knowing they had to endure many shots, along with necessary adjustments to have the honor of the hunt, I sincerely value them. Sometimes the corrections even required the heat of a flame in order to get a broadhead to sit aerodynamically true on the tip.

For those who desire to be a straight arrow for Christ, I have a feeling my shaft selection process has a sobering ring of familiarity. The testing, the heat of changing, and the patiently waiting in God's quiver until time to be sent to His target is not easy. For some, it will require slight adjustments. For others, some severe corrections are needed. Though it is a grueling procedure to withstand, the longing to be considered one of His "select arrows" remains.

God wants a quiver full of #1s. Allow Him to do what He must to write on your heart, "a select arrow." May the testing bring a deep joy in knowing He loves you enough to want you to be qualified to fulfill His divine purpose.

Lord, thank You that You have seen the hearts of humankind, yet You still choose to use us. You are the one-and-only Mighty Warrior. It is with an understanding of what is required in order to be one of Your usable arrows that I pray, "Make it so for me." I can now see that the times of testing I have already been through were part of the process. I pray for grace, strength, and mercy to go on with You as You adjust me, correct me, and straighten me to fly true to the places You will send me. In Your name I pray, amen.

15

A Sound
like a Frog

I climbed onto my ladder stand before daylight and settled in for a morning hunt. There was a sizable pond to my right, and the noises that came from it softly filled the area. One particular sound caught my ear and brought a smile to my face because it reminded me of one of my favorite stories…

> A little boy said to his grandpa, "Granddad, make a sound like a frog."
>
> His grandfather was sort of a rough old fellow and bluntly denied his grandson's request. However, the boy was not about to be refused.
>
> "Please, Granddad, make a sound like a frog!"
>
> "No!" came the old man's grouchy reply.
>
> "Oh, please, Granddaddy, make a sound like a frog."
>
> Exasperated with the little guy's persistence, the granddad asked, "Why?"
>
> " 'Cause Grandma says, 'When Grandpa croaks, we can all go to Six Flags!'"

It sounds like the grandpa had built a less-than-favorable reputation for himself. His legacy had apparently been established, and the assumption was that he would never change. This story makes me want to work on my memory. By that I don't mean my brain's ability to recall; rather, on how I will be remembered in the minds of others. May it never be that my wife, my children, grandchildren, or friends would ever grimace at the mention of my name.

According to Proverbs 10:7, the key to creating a memory that brings smiles to the faces of those around us is to allow righteousness to reign in our hearts. On the other hand, if we want our names to leave the taste of rottenness in the mouths of those who say them in the future, then all we have to do is embrace wickedness. Things that rot are eventually forgotten completely; they disappear into oblivion. However, Psalm 112:6 honors those who choose God's way with a lasting legacy: "For he will never be shaken; the righteous will be remembered forever."

A good goal for life would be that should the day arrive when we become grandparents, we will never hear any of our grandchildren say, "Granddad, make a sound like a frog."

Lord Jesus, hallowed be Your name. How sweet it is to remember it. Today I place my legacy into Your care. As I pursue Your pleasure, I know one of the benefits will be a sweet remembrance when my name comes to the minds of those who are close to me. Help me end my earthly journey with a reputation that honors both my name and, more importantly, Yours. It's in Your sweet name I pray, amen.

16

Skin and Ink

*Behold, I have inscribed you
on the palms of My hands.*
Isaiah 49:16

As my eyes carefully scan the woods in search of deer, my mind often works in overdrive on other matters. Sometimes it may be a business issue I'm working through, a home improvement or repair I'm planning, or something I need to say to someone. Though my body is sitting motionless, my brain is spinning with activity.

On occasion, something of incredible importance may cross my thoughts. I've learned through the years that to be safe, I must immediately write myself a note about it. If I don't, it's lost the moment I go on to something else. One solution that has spared me plenty of trouble has been to scribble my most important memos on the closest surface I can find. During the times when no paper is available, I use the meaty part of my palm as a notepad. That section of the hand seems to receive ink very well, and my critical notes rarely get erased.

This method works great, especially in the treestand, for two good reasons. One, slipping a glove down is a lot quieter and requires far less motion than digging through pockets for paper. All I need to retrieve is the pen I conveniently keep in my shirt pocket. Deer are less likely to be spooked by this minimum movement. Second, while a note may be written on paper, I may easily forget to take it out of my camo pants pocket when I get home. However, with an inscription of ink on the skin of my hand, it's at least a 99-percent guarantee that I will eventually see it since my hand rarely leaves my arm! Once home, when I see the note, I immediately recall how important it is and act on it.

Knowing the value I place on what I write on my hand, today's verse provides a great deal of comfort to my heart. What an incredible blessing to think that we are of so great importance to the God of all this universe that He would write us on His hand!

If you are one of those who uses the "skin and ink" method, the next time you are scribbling your thoughts on your epidermis, I hope a warm wave of joy washes over your soul as you recall, "Behold, I have inscribed you on the palms of My hands." In fact, it might even be a good idea for you to write His name on your skin from time to time!

Blessed Father, how grateful I am that You write notes about me on Your palms. To know I am not forgotten is a joy beyond measure. May I never forget You. To Your glory I pray in Christ's name, amen.

17

The Snort

As for all his adversaries, he snorts at them.

Psalm 10:5

In my 35 years of hunting the whitetail deer, I have had many occasions to be startled by their loud, unexpected snorting. It is especially shocking, for example, before daylight as I slip through the blackness of the predawn hour on my way to a stand. Unaware the deer are there and that my presence in their territory has been detected, I am, without exception, brought to my emotional knees when they make their displeasure known with a resounding nasal blast.

For whatever reason they do it, whether to intimidate a threatening intruder or to warn other deer of danger or to simply clear their "smeller," I am always rattled to the core by the noise. I suppose they are doing what comes naturally, but these sudden, ear-splitting sounds have taken years off my life.

Interestingly, in the Scriptures it is said that man has been known to snort. While the deer does it as an innocent, natural response, man is usually guilty of intentionally using it for an unholy reason. In the original language of Psalm 10:5, the word for snort, *puwach*, has the following connotations: puff, pant, scoff, or speak in a harsh manner. In most cases, it seems that a wicked man's snorting is an audible, outward sign of an inward case of pride and arrogance against the presence of righteousness. Also, it is often a reaction to those times when a person doesn't get his way. Deer likely snort in self-defense. Man, however, snorts in defense of self.

While a deer's snort is distinctively consistent in its sound, man's has various tones to it. It can take the form of a car horn blown by an irate driver. It might come out as profanity when a sore loser is being defeated in a sporting competition. Some snorts sound like malicious gossip intended to demean someone as a result of jealousy. At one time or another you have probably heard a human snort—never a pretty sound to hear or a sweet sound to make.

If we are honest, most of us have been guilty of a forceful, rude blast of pride. Sadly, we have probably done it without knowing what a shock it was to everyone nearby. The next time a startled, vocal deer shocks your socks off, let it remind you to be careful to control your mouth. After all, a snort is just hot air!

Lord, there have been times when I have been considered an enemy to the wicked and have heard their snorts. Thank You for delivering me from the painful effects of their anger. Knowing that scoffing at others is never a sweet sound, I pray that You will come alongside me and help me overcome arrogance in my own heart and avoid blasting others with it. Instead, make my words pleasant to hear in the ears of those around me. In Your name I pray, amen.

18

Song of the Hunter

I will sing to the LORD, because
He has dealt bountifully with me.
Psalm 13:6

One of the advantages of being alone on a deerstand is the opportunity to sing without worrying about hecklers. While the volume might have to be subdued because of the sensitive ears of game, we can deliver a melody and lyrics that never have to be subject to the unsolicited reviews of critics.

One particular type of song that is especially wonderful to sing on the stand is a worship tune. The audience is limited to one, and the Lord will always be impressed with our praise to Him. Psalm 33:1 is an encouraging passage, even for the roughest of voices: "Sing for joy in the LORD, O you righteous ones; praise is becoming to the upright." Even the rugged, untrained voices of the most burly hunters among us bring delight to the Lord. It happens when a song of praise rises from a righteous and grateful soul. No matter what tone is produced, as the vocal cords play the strings of the heart, God is pleased. His concern is "our hearts...not the *Billboard* charts!"

What is a good song for a glad heart to sing? Only the heart of the singer can know. For one, the words may tell of a passage on dry ground through some type of "Red

Sea": "He turned the sea into dry land; they passed through the river on foot; there let us rejoice in Him!" (Psalm 66:6). For another, they may sing at the realization of how the sky testifies to the awesomeness of its Maker: "The heavens are telling of the glory of God; and their expanse is declaring the work of His hands" (Psalm 19:1).

Songs with words that are written on grateful tablets of flesh are like snowflakes. No two are alike; each is always an original: "He put a new song in my mouth, a song of praise to our God" (Psalm 40:3).

Whatever your song may be, feel free to sing it in the silence of your deerstand. When you finish, sit quietly and listen—you just might hear the applause of one pair of hands. God will love your singing...that's a promise.

Today I lift my song of praise to You, O heavenly Father. It is one that You put in me. Please accept these words and music from my heart. It is my way of saying thank You for Your boundless love toward me. In Your name I pray, amen.

19

The Look

*They perish at the rebuke
of Your countenance.*
Psalm 80:16

Have you ever unintentionally wandered under another hunter's stand and ruined his hunt? I hate to admit it, but I've been guilty of that. I'll never forget the expression on the fellow's face when I happened to look up and see him glaring at me. The hunter didn't say anything; he just stared at me in disgust. The look on his unhappy face made me want to find a hole to crawl into.

That wasn't the first time I had been given a look of displeasure. It happened a few times in church when I was growing up. Sometimes as I sat on a pew lined with a bunch of teenagers we would pass notes, whisper, and create a distraction with our giggles.

Up front, in his chair that was elevated and just behind the pulpit, my dad's face would be red with embarrassment that his son was being so unruly. Disregarding how he looked to the congregation who could see him, the preacher would establish a hard-rock look on his face and set his eyes on me. With a stare that would melt cast iron, my dad would wait for me to look his way. Suddenly the blood would drain from my face when I locked eyes with him. There would be absolutely no doubt in my mind that the death sentence for my derriere would be handed down. That's when I would pass the note off to a friend, slither back into my chair, put my hands on my lap, and wait nervously for the last "amen" to be said.

I usually survived those unfortunate episodes, but not without some pain. Today, I'm the better for it. And being a dad myself I have had the chance to use those same discomforting stares on my own kids. If children are sensitive, a parent's facial warnings can be very effective. It worked for my mom and dad, and it's worked for me.

Dads are not the only ones who know how to accomplish something with a piercing facial expression. In today's verse the deplorable state of God's people is described and then the last line of the verse says, "They perish at the rebuke of Your countenance." Does that sound like all God had to do was look at them with displeasure? I have a feeling that when the people realized God saw them as a grievous reproach on His good name, those who cared about their relationship with Him melted with fear.

If we could see His face just once when we bring dishonor to His name, I suspect we would not delay the altering of our ways. The truth is, according to John 16:8, when the Holy Spirit came His work was to "convict the world concerning sin and righteousness and judgment." When our wayward hearts are suddenly pricked by the Spirit of God, we would do well to consider the warning. It is in that moment that the eyes of faith can behold the "rebuke" of God's countenance.

Our heavenly Father loved us enough to accept us the way we were when we came to Him as sinners. However, He loves us enough not to leave us that way. Just as my dad's stern look of vexation toward my misconduct in church was motivated by his care for my character, so is God's look of displeasure for our sinful behaviors an indication that He hopes for a change in our hearts.

Oh, God! My kind Redeemer and Lover of my soul, thank You for caring enough about me to draw me to Yourself. There are times when my actions must disappoint You. Forgive me, Lord, and cause me to act in such a way that Your face will not scowl but shine with a smile when You look at me. In Jesus' kind name, amen.

20

What to Wear?

Worship the LORD in holy attire.
Psalm 96:9

Picking the right outfit to wear in public is not one of my better gifts. It is for that reason that my wife, Annie, always has her eye on me as we prepare to leave the house. I can really relate to the comedian who said he was dressed to go out and was standing around waiting for his wife to finish. She walked by him, looked him up and down, and asked with a tone of disgust, "Are you going to wear that tonight?" The only response he could come up with was, "Oh, no, ma'am! I'm just wearin' this while I get ready!"

While I may not be gifted in the area of meeting the public in just the right threads, I believe I have developed the skills required to dress properly for a hunt. (If I approached my dressing for the public with the same effort I put into getting decked out for an archery deer hunt, I could easily end up on the cover of *GQ* magazine. Don't those initials stand for "game quota"?)

Why is clothing an issue in terms of hunting? It's necessary to blend in with the surroundings. Otherwise the highly gifted eyes of a deer can detect a person's presence and his chances for a shot fly out the window of opportunity. If I know, for example, my stand will be in the shadows of heavy, early season foliage, I choose a slightly darker pattern of camo. If more sunshine will be in the woods because the leaves have fallen, I might go the lighter-colored route. Basically, a deer hunter's attire has to be right—and I don't take the responsibility lightly.

Besides the woods, there is another place a hunter can go that requires far greater attention be given to what is worn. What we wear when we call on the name of God and enter into His presence is a very serious matter. Psalm 96:9 specifically lists what should cover us: "holy attire."

What is this holy attire? The righteousness of Christ. To go into the presence of God without it is spiritual disaster. Relying on our own good works leaves us dangerously exposed to God's intolerance of sin. Psalm 5:4 warns, "You are not a God who takes pleasure in wickedness; no evil dwells with You." Nothing good comes from our flesh. It is only corruption. However, thanks to God's provision of a "new self" created in the righteousness of His Son, we can "put Him on" (Ephesians 4:24) and go confidently into God's presence.

Hebrews 10:19,20 encourages us in this way: "Therefore, brethren, since we have confidence to enter the holy place by the blood of Jesus, by a new and living way which He inaugurated for us through the veil, that is, His flesh…" And Isaiah 61:10 is a wonderful comfort: "He has clothed me with garments of salvation, He has wrapped me with a robe of righteousness."

So when we are sitting on a deerstand in our proper attire or in church clothed in our Sunday-best, always remember this: Entry into God's presence is an incredible privilege, and we must be rightly clothed when we get there. Thankfully, Jesus is our attire. "Putting Him on" by faith ensures that when we meet God it is not us that He sees. Instead, it is His Son's righteousness that covers us.

"Are you dressed in the right attire?"

Blessed be Your name, Jesus, for doing what You did at the cross. May I be found in You, not having a righteousness of my own but only that which is through faith in You. You are blameless, and I am grateful that You allow weak and sinful people to call You Lord. Please cover me with Your finery. Without it I am doomed. Blessed be Your name, amen.

21

Prime Time

In the morning, O LORD, You will hear
my voice; in the morning I will order
my prayer to You and eagerly watch.

Psalm 5:3

As any deer hunter knows, there's hardly anything more exciting than to finally end the predawn journey to the stand by climbing in, sitting down, and waiting for legal shooting light. No matter how many times it's done, serious outdoorsmen long to do it again.

One thing I love to do after I buckle in, load up, and get my face mask in place is to offer a prayer for the time before me. After that, I put my ears and eyes in search mode. Today's verse reminds me of this process. The psalmist David's routine is perfect for the hunter who rises early. First of all, morning is when we seem fittest for prayer. Our minds are on full alert, we are fresh, and we hopefully have some good rest behind us. Also, we are not yet filled with the business of the day. The morning finds us as mentally uncluttered as we can be. It's a great time—and an important time—to go to the Lord for worship and guidance.

Second, with a clear head that comes with the morning, it is much easier to order our prayers to the Lord. Like well-placed arrows in the hands of a skilled archer, a steady mind can better direct the prayerful petitions of the heart. I am well aware of how spiritually groggy and muddled I can be by the end of a busy day. It's hard to concentrate on anything when the brain is tired and the soul has been beaten by the cares of life. For that reason, an early morning sit in a deerstand is even more important than may be realized.

Finally, David's attitude of "eagerly watching" is worthy of notice. What was he watching for? Knowing that God hates sin, the psalmist vigorously stands guard against entertaining iniquity. His desire to avoid being numbered among the boastful, the liars, the men of bloodshed and deceit drives him to finely tune his senses and start the morning prepared for anything. How well we all would do to follow this order.

If the stand is where you are headed this morning or where you are at this moment, this is prime time for prayer. Take advantage of it!

O Holy God, thank You that I am not alone in these woods. You are here with me, and I am grateful You hear my voice. I know You are a God who takes no pleasure in wickedness. Help me eagerly keep watch against it. Deliver me this day from evil. Lead me in Your righteousness and make Your ways straight before me. I bow my head in reverence to You. Blessed be Your name forever and ever. Amen!

22

Skipping in the Dark

For I, the LORD your God, will hold your right hand, saying to you, "Fear not, I will help you."

Isaiah 41:13 (NKJV)

There are very few parts of a deer hunt I dislike. Perhaps the untimely onslaught of gnats that seem to invade only when a deer is moving toward my stand would be on the list. (They must love adrenaline!) The sight of a passing pair of coyotes that scatters the deer herd leaving me with an early trip back to my truck is a bummer. These things are terribly bothersome, but there is another part of hunting I don't care for at all, even after 35 years in the woods. It's the early morning treks to the stand by myself in the pitch-black darkness of the predawn forest.

I'm always grateful when another hunter is along. Having company puts the joy back into the journey. Instead of being reduced to a shaky, tentative shuffle through the forest, the presence of a companion brings a lilt to my steps. The imagination that would be hindered by thoughts of a deadly attack by a cougar, a grizzly, or a bogeyman is freed instead to look forward to the hunt.

There is something familiar about how the presence of a friend squelches the struggle of moving alone through the blackness of the woods. It's the comfort that our heavenly Father gives to those who depend on Him for safety in this world. This is beautifully illustrated in the following poem by Lilah Lehman Gustafson. It is a true story told by a father to his little girl who had brought him comfort years before when he was facing a time of great testing. The verses were read at her father's funeral.

Skipping in the Dark

She trembled with fear as they entered the night
    To shadows like shrouds o'er the land
She whimpered, "I'm scared of the darkness ahead."
    He said, "Here, my child, hold my hand."
She offered hers up and she clasped it in his,
    Her wee little fist in his palm.
The strength of his grip, and the love in his touch
    To her quiv'ring heart brought a calm.
Her fears now allayed and her courage restored
    She bounced by his side with a lark.
And feeling the grasp of his hand on hers
    She said, "Look! I can skip in the dark!"
Her daddy looked down at his dear little girl,
    So trusting, so sure of his care.
For though she could not see the path in the dark,
    She feared not, for Daddy was there!

The Lord sent a message through his little girl
    That bolstered his own troubled mind.
"I ever am with you; I'll guard every step
    Wherever your pathway may wind.
For I am thy God, I will hold your right hand,
    Fear not, Dear One, I will help thee.

For I am continually here by your side
    Still holding your hand. Trust in Me."

With tears in his eyes, he looked up to the heav'ns;
    The stars gave brightness to night
God prodded his heart, "There's no darkness on earth
    Can ever extinguish the light.
Look up, hurting child, and give me your hand,
    There's light on your pathway so stark.
My hold will not fail, you're secure in my grasp;
    You, too, child, can skip in the dark."

Dear heavenly Father, thank You for Your confident hand that reaches for my own. Please let me feel the gentle squeeze of it on mine in the dark times of this life. I need Your guidance, Your confidence, and the light of Your love. With these, I, too, can skip in the night. In Jesus' comforting name I pray, amen.

23

Little Foxes and Big Toenails

Search me, O God, and know my heart....
See if there is any wicked way in me.

Psalm 139:23,24 (NKJV)

It's the little foxes that spoil the vines" is a familiar quip adapted from Song of Solomon 2:15. There's a ton of wisdom in this ounce of words! From the small, seemingly insignificant irritations that can eventually wreck a marriage to the constant-but-quiet drip of a leaky faucet that becomes a major distraction to our ability to concentrate, the applications are endless.

One important part of our spiritual lives to which "the little foxes" concept should be applied is in the way small sins, if ignored, can lead to accepting greater transgressions. To learn to be faithful in the lesser things is to become a ruler over greater things. The following true (and somewhat gross) story is a prime example from my own experience that illustrates how the Lord used the "little foxes" to alert me to the need to be on guard against even the tiniest of iniquities.

Back in the 70s I traveled with a band. One night, my partner, Ron, and I checked into a Mississippi motel after a concert. As Ron showered before retiring for the night, I took the opportunity to trim my toenails that were long overdue for a pedicure. Instead of placing the trimmings in a wastebasket, I was a slob and threw them at random across the room. My big toe nearly needed a chain saw to remove the unusually long growth. When I finally peeled the ugly thing off, I didn't even look up but just gave it a good fling.

The next morning as I showered, Ron made coffee with the in-room self-service machine. The wall-mounted appliance sat next to a shelf that held glass mugs. I decided to help myself to the brew, so I removed the pot and poured some into one of the cups that rested at eye level on the shelf. After I put the pot back, I began to sip the coffee. I remember making a comment about how good it tasted. Being a good enough blend to be consumed to the last drop, I turned up the cup to consume the remaining portion. That's when I saw it! There in the bottom of the mug was the huge toenail from my big toe that I had pitched the night before. I recognized its shape, but it was now much cleaner than I remembered. I nearly gagged. I was, to say the least, grateful that I'd chosen that cup and not Ron. Ron nearly split a gut when he learned why I was looking so pale.

I suppose I deserved what I got. As I reeled from my self-inflicted nausea, I'll never forget how these words came to my mind: "It's the little foxes..." Strangely enough, I felt a certain guilt for what I had done. I know that toenail tossing does not rank up there with the vilest of sins. While it may have been a small and even insignificant act, it was weighty in its potential. What I was really dealing with was the dangerous intent of my heart.

The evening before, I consciously knew that while I was flinging toenails, I was not doing unto others as I would have them do to me. I showed blatant disrespect for the motel owner, the person who would clean the room, Ron, and the next guest who would occupy the space I was in. (I could only imagine what would have happened had that individual found what I had discovered in the mug. It could have resulted in a nasty confrontation, even a lawsuit!)

As an act of penance, I tried to gather up as much of the toe debris as I could find. I left that motel a different man—perhaps not excelling to the point of sinless perfection, but at least having taken one small step toward righteousness. Oh, how I pray that God always gives me the ammunition of grace to shoot the little foxes!

Lord, thank You for loving me and being patient with me in my struggle to please You. I want to walk worthy of Your presence in my heart. Help me be on guard against the little sins that would come in and try to make my heart an unclean and unwelcome place for Your Spirit to dwell. In Jesus' name I pray, amen.

24

Safety Belt

He will not allow your foot to slip....
The LORD is your keeper.
Psalm 121:3,5

I seriously doubt if any hunter has deliberately jumped out of a treestand for the sole purpose of hurting himself. However, most of us have heard of people who have accidentally fallen and been maimed or even killed. Maybe you have experienced this type of accident (I hope not!). Regretfully, I can testify to the pain of an unplanned fall from a treestand. It's not fun!

Anyone who knows or can imagine how an unexpected plunge feels would never intentionally hurt himself this way. If he did he would have to be crazy! Yet when it comes to injuring our spiritual lives by diving into immorality, mankind can be incredibly dim-witted. Amazingly, lots of folks inflict a "sinjury" to their souls by jumping—not just falling—into transgression.

Consider the wake of painful sorrow that followed King David after his unholy tryst with Bathsheba (see 2 Samuel 11–12). The consequences he paid were extremely difficult:

> [Thus says the LORD God of Israel,] "Why have you despised the word of the LORD by doing evil in His sight?"…Now therefore, the

sword shall never depart from your house, because you have despised Me and have taken the wife of Uriah the Hittite to be your wife....Behold I will raise up evil against you from your own household; I will even take your wives before your eyes and give them to your companion....The child also that is born to you shall surely die (2 Samuel 12:9-11,14).

David's situation is fair warning for us all to understand this sobering truth: If a wayward thought is not "taken captive to the obedience of Christ," eventually a decision must and will be made. At some point the chance to sin can turn into a choice to sin. When the resulting pain of the consequences is ignored in advance and our feet leave the platform of holiness, the jump becomes "the fall." When the heart thuds against the hard ground of disobedience, that's when we suddenly realize how stupid we've been.

Smart treestand hunters always use a safety belt, even if they are the most cautious of climbers. I would argue that to consciously avoid using a tethering device that could stop a deadly fall is the same thing as deliberately putting yourself in harm's way. This is true because a hunter ascends the tree knowing the risks involved. The same is true for a person's spiritual walk. To not take advantage of the available safety measures when doing something that is inherently dangerous is asking for trouble.

The most modern example I can think of to illustrate this is found on most of our desks in our homes. Climbing into the innumerable branches of the Internet without a filter that blocks the smut sites is a mindless invitation to disaster. Like a belt that makes a hunter safe, an Internet filter protects a sin-sensitive user. The program doesn't falter when our will is weak. With millions of porno websites to log onto not strapping ourselves to a technical safety device that can effectively assist us with self-discipline is a sad disregard for the deadly dangers.

Are you uncomfortable acknowledging your weaknesses? If so, lean on 2 Corinthians 12:9 for strength: "My grace is sufficient for you, for power is perfected in weakness." To not admit how easy it is to be enticed by ungodly pleasures is the same as leaving your safety belt at home when you go into the tall timber to hunt.

The next time you stand at the bottom of a tree and look up in preparation to climb, remember to ask this probing question that applies to both body and soul: "Where's my safety belt?"

Father, thank You for being my mighty protector against a deadly fall into sin. I don't want to be unwise in my climb to heaven. Help me be brave enough to admit that I will always be in need of the safety of Your presence in my life. I know it is foolish to attempt any ascent while I am knowingly disconnected from Your grace. Bless Your name for caring enough about me to remind me of my great need for You. Hang on to me, God. In Jesus' name, amen.

25

Attacked!

Put on the full armor of God.
Ephesians 6:11

My friend Randy stopped his truck and said, "This is the place." The North Dakota farm had numerous good areas for hunting mule deer, and the one he had chosen was near a river. Before I exited the vehicle, we agreed on a time he would return to pick me up. The sun was yet to rise and the warm, August bow-season morning was already in the low 80s.

As his taillights disappeared into the distance, I stood in the dark and fastened the four snaps of my sleeve guard. As I did, I suddenly heard a strange sound. It was an eerie hum, sort of high pitched and growing in volume as the seconds passed. I dug for my flashlight. I didn't want to turn it on and risk alerting the deer that the truck had deposited a human being in their territory, but I had to find out what the source of the noise was. When I flicked the light on, what I saw was unbelievable. I was quickly being covered by a thick swarm of mosquitoes. Their troops were innumerable. Realizing I was under serious attack, I immediately abandoned what was to be the first morning of deer hunting in North Dakota and started a brisk walk in the direction of camp. Within 45 minutes the light of the little trailer was in view. When I opened the door, Randy was quite surprised to see me. I was happy to be safely inside and alive.

"I could have died out there!" I blurted. When I explained my dilemma, Randy didn't disagree with my assessment. His only response was, "Are you going back out there?"

"You bet I am, good buddy. I didn't come all the way to North Dakota to be whipped by a few million pesky, pistol-packin' skeeters!" I disappeared into the bedroom, then came out with my "armor" on: Two pairs of pants, two shirts, two pair of gloves, and an extra face mask. Of course, in the temperatures of the late-summer western plains, the extra clothes made me feel like I was hunting in a sleeping bag inside a sauna. This meant I simply had to make sure the wind was always in my face and I had plenty of water along to replenish my fluids.

The pests swarmed fiercely and made plenty of racket around my ears, but not one of their drills made it through my covering! As I monitored a well-used pass-through area that led from one field to another, I felt completely safe. The day ended without another single drop of my blood being donated to the bellies of those thirsty creatures. And I managed to bring home a nice mulie. It was some of the best meat I've ever eaten because I won the "war."

Satan also wages a war against us—a spiritual battle that daily challenges the souls who belong to Christ. The enemy and his swarms of schemes would destroy us if we allowed them to. They are constantly on the attack. The good news is that we have protection! There is a suit of armor available to each of us to wear:

> For our struggle is not against flesh and blood,
> but against the rulers, against the powers,
> against the world forces of this darkness,
> against the spiritual forces of wickedness in
> the heavenly places.

Therefore, take up the full armor of God, so that you will be able to resist in the evil day, and having done everything, to stand firm. Stand firm therefore, having girded your loins with truth, and having put on the breastplate of righteousness, and having shod your feet with the preparation of the gospel of peace; in addition to all, taking up the shield of faith with which you will be able to extinguish all the flaming arrows of the evil one. And take the helmet of salvation, and the sword of the Spirit, which is the word of God. With all prayer and petition pray at all times in the Spirit, and with this in view, be on the alert with all perseverance and petition for all the saints (Ephesians 6:12-18).

How foolish it would have been for me to go back to the outdoors that morning in North Dakota without the protective covering I wore. Those mosquitoes would have drained me dry in a matter of minutes. It would be just as senseless to attempt to win the war against the devil without proper battle attire. While God's armor might present a little extra weight to carry, we cannot win without it.

Will you suit up?

Father, thank You for providing the equipment I need to fight and win the battle for righteousness. Please guide me to the armor room. Help me don each piece and secure it firmly. I need Your strength to fight and to carry the weight of this suit of armor. Thank You. In Jesus' name, amen.

26

Whiter than Snow

Wash me, and I shall be whiter than snow.

Psalm 51:7

Nearly 100 percent of the uncles, aunts, and cousins on the Chapman side of my family have snow-white hair. An in-law once quipped at a Chapman reunion, where the room was full of Chapmans, "This place looks like a big box of Q-tips!" He was right.

I was not spared this trait. As a hunter, my glow-in-the-dark head of hair is a potential hazard. I usually put a mask over my entire head the moment I exit the truck and walk toward my stand, even in the dark of the predawn hour. I'm just sure that a deer's incredible night vision can pick me up as I slip along. In their eyes, without my head covering I would appear to be a mysteriously illuminated globe bobbing by. Even I would be spooked at a sight like that!

Not only do I cover up in order to salvage my deer hunt, I also do it for safety's sake. Since my hair is the same color as some of a deer's fur, like its tail, I rarely remove my mask while I'm in the woods. I wouldn't want a hunter to shoot me and have to check me in at the local hospital.

Though it requires careful attention and constant concealment, in no way do I resent or dislike my "cotton" top. This is true for several reasons. One, I may not be smart but at least I can look like I have the wisdom garnered by time. Two, if I ever get lost in the wilderness, the helicopter pilot can spot me a lot quicker. A third reason to embrace (hold onto!) my frosty flocks is a more recent discovery.

Annie and I were traveling and stopped at a McDonald's restaurant for a quick break and some coffee. I went to the counter and ordered two cups, then met Annie at the car.

"Annie," I announced in amazement, "you wouldn't believe how cheap the coffee is here. I got two cups for 50 cents. Unbelievable!"

As we drove away I noticed Annie looking at me with a silly grin on her face.

"What?" I inquired.

"You have no idea what just happened in there do you?"

"What?" I asked again.

"They gave you the senior discount!" Her laugh was disturbing.

I was appalled at first. I thought about turning around to see if I could get the manager to fire the little snit that undercharged me. However, as I thought about how much savings my new status might represent, I calmed down. So the third reason is appreciating my "seasoned appearance."

The primary reason I am satisfied with my white hair comes back to me when I look in the mirror. Years ago, when I noticed my "pepper" was turning to salt, I found a good way to deal with the impact it was having on my ego. At that time, I was a young Christian and eager to see the Lord in whatever way He would reveal Himself. As the deep-brown hue of my mane began to seriously pale, I decided I could look at it as a constant reminder of how God was kind enough to take my sin-blackened heart, wash it in the red, redeeming blood of Christ, and make it white as snow. It was a transforming decision.

From that era on, I never fought it. I've never had the desire to restore the original color with the liquid youth that comes from a bottle. (Annie said, "Steve, why dye it, it's already died!")

If you are also pigment challenged, count your blessings. Right there on your noggin is the story of the gospel of Christ. Cover it when you deer hunt, but let your light shine when you're not in the woods!

Father, thank You for white hair. Perhaps it is a man's glory not just because it represents the distance he might have traveled in time or the wisdom he has gained, but because it reflects the story of Your love for us. Knowing that You number the hairs on our heads, would You be so kind as to sustain my total? Bless You. Amen.

27

Popsicles

Each one is tempted when he is carried away
and enticed by his own lust.
James 1:14

Have you ever been so cold that your fingers and toes became numb? What is especially interesting is how the numbing process is so gradual. As the warm air is slowly replaced by the cold, we sit there oblivious to the change. Then all of a sudden there's a stinging pain. The stiffness makes it hard to regain comfort. We try to wiggle our toes, but they won't move quickly enough. We blow warm air into our gloves to ward off the throb. Usually by then it's too late; the damage has been done.

Many years ago I heard a story about an ancient tribe of Arctic dwellers. They used the numbing effect of ice to destroy the wolves that were coming into their camps and killing their valuable dogs and other animals.

The hunters would coat a knife blade with the fresh blood of an animal, let it freeze, then repeat the same thing over and over until the sharp steel was concealed by a thick covering of frozen blood. Then they would stick it into the ground, handle down and blade exposed upward. When the wolf's well-trained nose would find the enticing, flavorful "Popsicle" trap it would begin to lick it. As the wolf's tongue slowly numbed, the smell of the blood drove him to keep licking. By the time it licked down to the finely sharpened blade, its tongue would be so deadened by the ice that the wolf didn't know the blade was slicing its tongue to shreds. Wounded, the predator would wander away and likely starve to death.

While this method of hunting is unusually cruel, it is effective. The way intense cold sneaks up and wreaks havoc is a good picture of a spiritual truth. Through habitual sin, the "skin of our spirit," can be numbed, which eventually can block our ability to feel the "godly sorrow that leads us to repentance" (2 Corinthians 7:10). How many of us have given in to sordid hungers and were slowly numbed by them, so much so that we kept consuming until our "tongues" reached the blade of destruction—and sometimes continued until death.

Why don't you stop for a moment in this bitterly cold world we live in and carefully consider what you are consuming? Are you licking with a frenzy on any "Popsicles"? If so, ask God to help you now and renew your sensitivity to His leading.

O Lord, I'm grateful that You can help me avoid being numbed by sin. Deliver me today from the trap of Satan's enticements. I pray for Your wisdom and strength to be able to see them and flee from them. Please hear my cry. Thank You. In Jesus' name, amen.

28

The Fawn

I am the good shepherd.

John 10:11

It's hard to explain the depth of feelings that filled my heart when a Wildlife Resources agent put a spotted fawn in my arms. He had found it abandoned, sickly, and scared. Hoping to nurse it back to a condition that would ensure good health, he was giving it the best care he could. The opportunity to hold the little fellow was a priceless moment for me. The spindly legged, wild infant seemed almost human in its appreciation for the contact with another living creature. As it sucked vigorously from the bottle in my hand, I had to wonder if survival was in the future for the young deer.

Annie was with me that day. She got to feed the little guy, too. As we drove away from the very memorable experience, she brought up an issue that was haunting.

"Steve, have you ever read John 10:11-13 in light of human children?" she asked.

I answered with a curious, "No."

Annie took her Bible from her travel bag and turned to the passage. "That fawn back there somehow makes me think of this passage. Listen":

> I am the good shepherd; the good shepherd
> lays down His life for the sheep. He who is a

> hired hand, and not a shepherd, who is not the owner of the sheep, sees the wolf coming, and leaves the sheep and flees, and the wolf snatches them and scatters them. He flees because he is a hired hand and is not concerned about the sheep.

Annie was nearly in tears as she said, "Even though that agent is doing what he can to care for that little fawn, there's no way he can love it like its mother can. He might feed it and keep it alive, but that's about it. He can't teach it the ways of the wild. Only its mother can do that. That little scared thing reminds me of far too many kids these days who are taken to daycare centers and left with babysitters. Those folks may very well care for those children, tend to them, and see to it they are alive at the end of the day. But when real trouble comes, like needing to discipline and train a defiant little spirit, guess who gets shortchanged? The hired hand does not 'own' the child. By nature, caretakers can't pour themselves into a child's life—at least not like a mother will."

The van was quiet for a long moment as the sobering thought of what Annie had just presented soaked into my heart. She was right. This nation's children, not all of them of course, but so many, are being raised by hired hands. Though the "paid-for parent" might indeed care for the child, there's no way he or she will deeply love him or her like a parent will. It's just not possible.

Annie and I discussed our fears of what the result will be when our unnurtured generation begins to have children of their own. The cash paid for outside caregivers will in no way compare to the cost we'll pay for living in a nation filled with parents who do not know why and how to love their own offspring. May God deliver us from passing on the heritage of abandonment.

O merciful Father, thank You that You have not lost any of Your children. Show me today how I can help change the trend of surrogate parenting. Though children may be in a room full of others like them, they must feel lost without the continual warmth and presence of a parent's love. Somewhere deep inside, they feel the loneliness and are afraid. I pray for the moms and dads who are making decisions that they might take into consideration their children. May You help every parent make wise choices when it comes to requirements and commitments of time. God, until our children find safe haven in You, keep the wolves away. I pray this in Jesus' name, amen.

29

The Trail

That the generation to come might know,
even the children yet to be born, that they
may arise and tell them to their children.

Psalm 78:6

I had cleared the trail to one of my favorite stand locations two years earlier, and it was time to do it again. Restoring it to a path that would ensure a quiet, undetected walk to the tree I would use required a rake for the layers of leaves that had fallen. Also, some trimming of the new growth of overhanging branches was necessary. After about an hour, I was standing under the familiar tree that held the sturdy platform. I carefully checked each step as I ascended and climbed in for a moment's rest.

It was quiet except for the mid-August mosquito buzzing at my ear. I surveyed the shooting lanes around the stand. They needed a little work, too. Before climbing down to complete the job, I looked over the trail that snaked off into the woods. I was satisfied it was ready for the upcoming season.

This trail had some good memories attached to it. I replayed the scene when a buck that had eluded me on several occasions came within 20 yards of my stand. The crunch of the leaves that alerted me to his presence echoed in my head. I could almost feel the slight sting of the kisser button sliding across my lower lip as the string was released. The snap of the bow limbs and the crashing sound as he ran off came rushing in. I could even feel the deep, nervous sigh that followed the shot. I recalled how it seemed to take minutes before I could exhale. It was an incredible moment. Isn't it great how memories can bring joy to our hearts?

As I climbed down and headed to my truck, I thought of my freshly cleared trail. Back there was a stand that was not just a platform at a "honey hole." It was a monument that honored the wonderful memories of seasons passed. I couldn't wait for the first day of season when I could follow my homemade path back to that special spot.

Trails are that way. They lead to destinations we long for and places we enjoy going back to. Besides my tree-stand trail, there's another one I love to travel: the trail that winds through time on my way to heaven. There's an awesome destination waiting for every believer! But there are places on this trail that I love to wander back to. The spot that means the most to me is best described in this lyric about my grandfather.

One Man Prayed

Back behind on the trail of time
There is a place that is sacred to me
Sometimes I go there in my mind
And I look upon it thankfully.

'Cause it was there long before my years
That a man whose blood runs through my veins
Fell on his knees and he said with tears
"God save my soul in Jesus' name."

That was the place, that was the time
When amazing grace came into my bloodline
And my soul was forever changed
When one man prayed in Jesus' name.

If time goes on further down the trail
Others will be born, and born again
And if I'm around I'll be sure to tell
How it came to pass that grace came in.

That was the place, that was the time
When amazing grace came into my bloodline
And so many souls were forever changed
'Cause one man prayed in Jesus' name.

Take a moment and think about your life. Where is
your path taking you? What has happened behind you
that means the most? Consider the things you do and
how they will affect those who come down the trail
behind you.

*Lord, thank You and bless You for meeting my ancestors on
this trail through time. I'll be forever grateful that the choice
they made for You not only changed their lives but mine as
well. Help me to be careful in my heart to keep on this way to
heaven, especially for the sake of those who follow. And until I
get home to be with You, I need the light of Your love to guide
me. In Jesus' name, amen.*

30

Apple Seeds

*The earth brought forth vegetation,
plants yielding seed after their kind, and trees bearing
fruit with seed in them, after their kind;
and God saw that it was good.*

Genesis 1:12

Whenever snacktime arrives while sitting in a deerstand, one of the best treats a hunter can take out of his pack is a fresh apple. The natural sugar is a boost, and the unique taste can wake the sleepiest of heads. Also, the aroma could very well get the attention of the sensitive nose of a hungry deer, enticing it into range.

Because this fruit is a familiar food to whitetails in this part of the country, I usually don't consume the entire apple. Instead, I save enough on the core to ensure it has plenty of pulp to give off a pleasing odor. I then put it under my boot and quietly smash it. Using the grated floor of the stand, I let the sweet-smelling debris fall through it to the earth below.

Whenever I crush an apple this way, I know that along with the ground-up meat of the fruit, the seeds fall to the soil as well. I've wondered if someday, years in the future, others will be able to track my stand locations by finding apple trees that have grown up in nondescript places in the middle of the woods!

If my stand has a solid floor, I do something a little different. Before consuming the apple, I take out my pocketknife and slice it in half. I'll eat one side and cut up the rest in small pieces and toss them out around me. Sometimes before I partake, I look at the nicely sliced halves and observe the exposed seeds. I like to do this because of a profound quip I heard several years ago: "You can count the seeds in an apple, but you can't count the apples in a seed."

An amazing amount of truth is packed into these few words. I find them especially inspiring when the opportunity arises to share the good news of the gospel of Christ with a group of young people. To think that even though I may be speaking to a few individuals who can be quickly counted, they in turn could bear spiritual fruit and possibly affect many others through the years. Sunday school teachers and camp counselors, for example, will be encouraged if they remember this truth when they get weary in well doing.

The potential of divine multiplication is even more heartening when I consider the fact that in my own home there once were two youngsters. They are now grown and on their own, but while they were with us Annie and I were careful to present Christ to them. It was truly exciting when each one of them confessed Jesus as Lord and Savior. While they are "just two," there's no way to calculate the eventual influence their testimonies might have on other people.

If you have an apple with you, open it up. Take a look at the little black dots inside. Count them. Remember, you are holding not just one seed but many apples that could feed many people and animals. Who could number them? The final tally is known only to God. Keep this in mind the next time the opportunity comes to share the good news of Jesus!

Father in heaven and maker of the apple trees and seeds, thank You for the way a seed can carry so much life. I pray for Your courage to seize every opportunity to share the gospel of Your Son. Though my audience may be small and quickly numbered, You can use them to reach others with Your love. Yours is the only love that deserves to go on through time. In Jesus' name, amen.

31

Words

*Every careless word that people speak, they shall give an
accounting for it in the day of judgment.*

Matthew 12:36

Another Friday came and it was time for the Chapmans
to travel again. Though I would have enjoyed a trip to the
woods for a leisurely hunt, I went along with the idea of
having a job as we loaded the van and headed to the airport.

The call to board was made, and we took our seats
toward the front of the cabin and settled in. I was next
to the window, Annie was in the middle, and the kids
occupied the aisle seats. Suddenly Annie nudged me
gently in the ribs and gave me that *Quick! Look-over-my-
shoulder-at-something-important* nod. When I leaned my
head around to take a peek, I was visibly taken aback.

Standing in the aisle right between Nathan and
Heidi, waiting for other passengers to fill the overhead
bins with their stuff, was a musician we had only seen
on TV. If I gave the name most would know it. He
(that narrows it down) was a highly flamboyant artist,
and his fame was well established in the marketplace. I
nearly gasped at how striking he looked in his dark,
long, flowing overcoat. The sunglasses were quite impres-
sive. And the ring on his hand must have weighed in at a

hefty 12 pounds. It sparkled like a spider web in the bright morning sun.

Annie and I didn't bring him to the attention of our children. Nathan was about ten and Heidi was around seven. We knew they would know who he was. We also knew that they had seen and heard our comical comments and expressions about him whenever he was gracing our TV set. To avoid their excited chatter, we both held our breath as the man passed.

What happened next was totally unexpected. Before they closed the door of the plane, Annie got a tap on the shoulder. It was the well-dressed woman who had followed the celebrity onboard.

"Hi! I'm _____, _____'s wife, and he would like to meet the two of you."

Needless to say, we were completely bewildered that he would remotely know who we were. Both of us felt totally unprepared, but to be nice we complied. In the mental chaos of the moment we forgot how we had acted when we had seen this man on TV in the secrecy of our den. We asked, "Nathan, Heidi, do you want to go with us?" Little did we know that we had just invited trouble to accompany us to the back of the cabin.

As we were being quite properly introduced, Nathan's eyes got bigger than fried eggs. I could tell he wanted to say something, but my brain couldn't register what it might have been. When it came his turn to shake the hand with the diamond-studded ring, Nathan spoke up in a voice that filled the airplane up to ten aisles away on both sides. "Oh! Mom and Dad! Isn't this the guy you always make fun of?"

Needless to say, I wanted to crawl into the overhead bins above me. No, better yet, I wanted the rapture to happen! I could feel my knees grow weak, and my pulse begin to falter. Annie sort of jerked as if she had been hit with a stun gun. It was awful. Annie is much "quicker on her feet" than I am. As Nathan's query dangled in the air like a wrecking ball, she made a valiant attempt to salvage our reputation. "Don't kids say the darndest things? He's just being silly." She and I both knew it wasn't Nathan who looked silly. We were caught red-tongued. Oh, how it hurt.

I'm not sure if he (the artist) or we (the dummies) ever fully recovered from that encounter. One thing is for sure, we learned two huge lessons that day. One, if you don't want it repeated, don't say it in front of kids. And two, it would always be smart to obey the instructions given in Ephesians 4:29. They are there not just to fill space on a page but for the good of us all. To heed them could spare a soul from a lot of grief!

> Let no unwholesome word proceed from your mouth, but only such a word as is good for edification according to the need of the moment, so that it will give grace to those who hear.

Forgive my mouth, Father, for sometimes I use it before engaging my brain! In Jesus' name, amen.

32

And So
They Prayed

Devote yourselves to prayer, keeping alert
in it with an attitude of thanksgiving.

Colossians 4:2

Whenever I deer hunt with my muzzle loader, I usually think about the story in the following lyric. It's a ballad set in the era of the Civil War.

And So They Prayed

A young golden-haired soldier stood in the ranks of
the brave
And the captain said, "Guns to the shoulder!"…and
they quietly marched away.

His blue eyes once thrilled his mother, but now they
were filled with fear
As he heard the cannon's thunder, and the field of
the battle drew near.

But in that moment, far away, a mother whispers,
"Amen."
'Cause she thought of her son and so she prayed,
and O how she prayed for him.

His young hands, once they were steady, when he'd
hunt by his father's side

But now they trembled as he readied his gun, and
    the enemy came into sight.

But in that moment far away, a father whispers,
    "Amen."
'Cause he thought of his son and so he prayed, and
    O how he prayed for him.

How quickly his legs once carried him, when he'd
    run with his sister to town
But he could not run from the bullet within, and so
    he fell to the ground.

But in that moment far away, a sister says, "Amen."
'Cause she thought of her brother, and so she
    prayed, and O how she prayed for him.

Well the letter arrived, it was stained with blood, and
    it was sadly received
And gathering around were the ones he loved, and
    they began to read.

But in that moment far away, a young soldier whis-
    pers, "Amen."
'Cause he thought of his family who would hear of
    his wounds, and so he prayed for them

O how he prayed for them
'Cause he knew they must have been praying for
    him.

Besides making an attempt to capture the emotions a
soldier might face during the horrors of battle, I had an
alternative motive in telling this story. I was taught by my
parents to always be alert to those moments when a loved

one comes to mind unexpectedly. To ignore the sudden thoughts might mean overlooking the move of the Holy Spirit to pray for that person. That's what the family in the song did for the soldier, and that's what I want to do as well.

Perhaps you have never considered using unanticipated thoughts of your loved ones as a cue to pray for them. All kinds of wars are being waged in the hearts of humans. A child at school, a spouse at home or at work, or a friend in a faraway place might be facing a spiritual battle. Is it beyond God's ability to move one person to pray for another? Certainly not! Today as you hunt, be on the alert for God bringing someone to mind whom you can lift up in prayer.

Lord, thank You for helping me be attentive to Your Holy Spirit. If there is one soul I can especially pray for today, please bring his or her name to my heart. Help me be a faithful watchman for the signal to lift a loved one to You. In Jesus' name, amen.

33

Fall Blend

A time to plant...

Ecclesiastes 3:2

I felt a little strange as I sowed the highly palatable mix of deer-friendly forages in the middle of August. It didn't feel right. Being a latecomer to the science of farming, I held a preconceived notion that the time to plant was only in springtime. But the seeds I was broadcasting were specifically developed for autumn growth. Still, it was hard to believe the message on the label of the two-and-half-pound bag: "Fall blend: best results if sown from mid-August to mid-September."

The instructions on that sack of seed was a pleasant but puzzling discovery for this new farmer. To be sure of the facts, I asked my expert-gardener wife, Annie, if this was normal. She informed me that certain flowers, such as tulips, mums, and her favorite, the hyacinth, can safely and effectively be planted after summer has passed. My perception about springtime and harvest was delightfully changed, and I gladly accepted the exceptions to the rules.

There's a certain comfort that can be drawn from this truth about autumn planting. And it's a consolation not just for the hunter who wants to create a tasty food plot to entice wary deer into range, but also for newly converted parents who have grown children. Only recently did I notice that a season is not mentioned in today's well-known verse, only "a time" to plant. As a result of coming to Christ later in years, the opportunity parents had to sow the seeds of the Scriptures into their children's hearts when they were young might have passed. With children who are beyond the springtime of their lives, to understand that fall planting is perfectly fine is great solace.

It wasn't until his later years that Paul, the apostle, was drastically changed from a persecutor of the saints to a champion of the cause of Christ. Moses was chosen in his fortieth year to lead God's people. Zacchaeus, the tax collector, met with salvation as an adult when he encountered the compassionate Christ. Somewhere in the hearts of these men were the divinely prepared soft spots where a seed could be sown. The same is true for adults today. Whether you are a mom or dad who is a latecomer to the kingdom of God or a longtime believer, there is hope since it is never too late for planting. May God bless you as you open your container of seed (the Scriptures) and seize the opportunity to sow into the hearts of your eye-level children in any season.

O, God! I have missed the spring season of sowing Your Word into my children's hearts. How grateful I am that it can also be done in the fall. I pray for opportunities to plant You in their lives. I trust You to soften the ground in their souls to receive You. In Jesus' name, amen.

34

Pick a Spot

Forgetting what lies behind and reaching
forward to what lies ahead...
Philippians 3:13

My new, whisper-quiet recurve worked beautifully as I came to full draw and released a cedar shaft arrow at the heavy doe below me. Unfortunately, my brain wasn't working as well as my bow. The arrow flew over the deer's back. So did the second shot. The third dug into the ground under her belly, and the fourth sailed to who knows where.

I couldn't believe it. Four golden opportunities royally blown. As the deer wandered off and left me bleeding profusely from the wounds in my ego, I began to mentally replay the misses to determine what I had done wrong. It didn't take but a minute of pondering my poor performance to come up with the answer. Without a doubt, I had allowed the presence of a real deer to get the best of me. As a result, I committed a fatal error. I failed to *pick a spot*. Instead of honing in on a tuft of hair or a shadow behind the deer's shoulder blade, I let the animal become a silhouette. Consequently, I left the tree with an empty quiver and a tag that would not be filled.

As disgusting and frustrating as failures can be, there's always something to learn from them. This bungled opportunity was no different. My inability to key in on a specific target on the deer's body was a product of forsaking the basics. That error can be corrected with experience; however, the other reason I squandered the chance for success will be much harder to overcome. And to tell you what that is requires a confession.

I was yet to score with traditional equipment. I consider it one of a deer hunter's greatest challenges. So to put it simply, I wanted to be able to brag to my wife, my hunting buddies, and to all who would hear me gloat, "I did it! Me! Me! I got a recurve kill!" I was so wrapped up in being able to tout success that I couldn't hold on to the rudiments of taking a shot. My ability to focus was destroyed by my pride. I had no plans for humility; as a result, humility is what I got.

How often in the rest of life do we face this same dilemma? For example, in an effort to impress their business partners some people forget the foundational principles of good ethics. Shots that completely miss the mark of good morals include shady deals and under-the-table trades for the sake of bolstering the bottom line.

In Philippians 3, the apostle Paul gives us the best advice regarding how to hone in on a specific target. It works for bowhunters *and* believers. First, "forgetting what lies behind": ignoring, as Paul did, the reputation of previous successes. He abandoned the desire to protect the pride that accompanies accomplishment. Second, he "reached forward to what lies ahead": in the same way a traditional shooter points his extended arm at the target, Paul directed his gaze to obeying Christ. With his eyes fixed on Jesus alone, he found his "spot" (see Hebrews 12:2).

I can't wait until next archery season to try my recurve again. Until then, I have to work on my skills as a shooter and the attitude of my heart. My plan is to adopt Paul's fine example for hitting the target: *Forget* and *reach*. I have a feeling it's going to work!

Lord, bless You for being longsuffering with me. Too often I have focused on the wrong things. Help me concentrate on obedience, not success. Help me keep the basics before me. And until I am safe with You, I will continually aim for the mark of being Christ-minded. In Jesus' name, amen.

35

He Never
Did Anything

*They shouted back, "Crucify Him!" But Pilate
said to them, "Why, what evil has He done?"
But they shouted all the more, "Crucify Him!"*
Mark 15:13,14

Two years ago I had the unforgettable opportunity of
singing in a midwestern prison. I'll never forget the
strange feelings I had when I entered the facility with the
chaplain and the doors slid back into their secure, locked
positions behind us. It was lunchtime, and the halls were
filled with men who moved in an orderly fashion toward
the eating area. Some smiled, some said hello, and others
looked quite somber as they passed. I cannot imagine
being confined in the way these men were. Being an avid
outdoorsman, I think if I were locked up I would probably wear one of those expressionless faces when I passed
visitors in the hall.

Sometimes when I'm headed down the open highway
on a drive to hunt or sitting in the quiet of a treestand
looking out through the wild of the woods, I think of
those men. I can see the faces of the ones who sat on the
first row of the pews in the chapel. How many of the
guys that filled the room that day would give nearly anything to be in the freedom of my boots? All of them.
When they come to mind, I pray for them.

I can recall the chaplain's description of how one particular thing kept many of the inmates emotionally

strong. It was their intense hope that their innocence would soon be confirmed and result in their release. He relayed how so many of the men would dive headlong into studies of the law in order to find a loophole or legal precedent that would work in their favor.

When a man is behind bars and is convinced of his innocence, the sorrow must run even deeper. It would take a man like this to better understand the injustice served to Christ as Pilate handed down the sentence of death to the Savior. One such gentleman, a prisoner in the state of Ohio, came to grips with how Jesus must have felt. James Alley maintains that he was accused, tried, convicted, and punished for doing nothing. As an inmate, James prays that someday his case will be retried with fairness. But he's not just a prisoner; James is also a talented lyricist. One day I was privileged to receive one of his songs in the mail. When I learned about his situation, the following lyric became even more meaningful. As you read it, see if you can feel James' emotion as he closely relates to his Savior.

He Never Did Anything

There's an angry crowd outside the city walls
And they're cursing at a man hanging on a cross
They're saying to Him, "Save Yourself if You're a
    king!"
But He was blameless as a lamb, He never did
    anything

Chorus
He never did anything but come to save the lost
He never did anything but pay the final cost

He healed the sick, raised the dead, and took away
the sting
But when it came to finding fault in Him, He never
did anything

When there's an angry storm that grows inside of me
I put my trust in the One who calmed the angry sea
And when I'm lonely He makes my sad heart sing
How could they ever crucify Him, He never did any-
thing

Although your flesh is enjoying the freedom of your deerstand and the open spaces of the great outdoors, do you feel "locked up" in your soul? Perhaps it's because you have been wrongly accused of something and you feel bound by the injustice. Or is there some other emotion that makes you feel like a prisoner? If so, take this opportunity to appreciate what Christ went through for you. My favorite part of James' candid lyric is his readiness to take his loneliness and sorrow to the one who was killed in spite of His innocence. Let James' example remind you to go to Christ in prayer with your gratitude for the sacrifice of His innocence for your sins. If you will, the storm might subside, and your joy may return.

Bless You, Father, for the freedom I have to bring my burden of bondage to You. As I cast my cares upon You, deliver me from my accusers. And until I am released from this injustice, I will trust You to be my most treasured companion in this place. In the name of Your innocent Son I come to You, amen.

36

Twice Amazed

Now when Jesus heard this, He marveled.

Matthew 8:10

The incredible sights of nature often leave me speechless. From incredible sunrises and brilliant white stars that dance in the night skies to uniquely colored patterns on butterfly wings and shades of gray in foggy morning ponds, I have had many opportunities to feel the sensation of wonder. I love those moments.

As much emotional depth and height that the sensation of awe holds for us who observe nature, it seems reasonable to assume that Jesus would have felt constantly amazed. After all, He is the Son of the one and only God who created all that intrigues us. However, in a Sunday sermon by Pastor Bill Rudd from Michigan, he noted that in all of the Gospels it is said that Jesus was only twice amazed. And in both instances it had nothing to do with the natural wonders of the universe. Instead, it had only to do with the human heart in relation to faith.

In Matthew 8, the centurion came to Jesus and requested that He heal his paralyzed servant. Feeling totally undeserving that Christ would enter his home, the centurion said in verses 8 and 9:

> Lord, I am not worthy for You to come under
> my roof, but just say the word, and my ser-
> vant will be healed. For I also am a man

under authority, with soldiers under me; and
I say to this one, "Go!" and he goes, and to
another, "Come!" and he comes, and to my
slave, "Do this!" and he does it.

It was following the centurion's stated understanding
of Jesus' ultimate authority, that Jesus marveled.

The second recording that shows Jesus' amazement is
found in Mark 6, when Jesus was in His hometown. The
people were astonished by His teaching, yet they ques-
tioned His wisdom and His miracles. They said, "Is not
this the carpenter, the son of Mary, and brother of James
and Joses and Judas and Simon? Are not His sisters here
with us?" As a result, it is noted in verse 5: "And He could
do no miracle there except that He laid His hands on a
few sick people and healed them." In verse 6 it is revealed,
"And He wondered at their unbelief."

In these two cases it was both the great amount of
faith and the lack of it that caused Christ to express His
amazement. The two extremes got His divine attention.

Do you understand and embrace the absolute
authority of the risen Christ and His ability to command
all that is seen and unseen? Meditate on Jesus' wisdom
and miraculous, healing touch.

*Oh amazing Jesus, I come in Your name. I am awed by Your
great wisdom, Your unparalleled authority, and the miracle of
redemption You so lovingly supplied at the cross. I bow my
heart before You and, with trembling flesh at the very thought
of it, I look forward to the day I can behold Your face. Until
then, may You always make me worthy of Your presence in my
heart. Amen.*

37

Straight to
the Pantry

*Enter His gates with thanksgiving and His courts
with praise. Give thanks to Him, bless His name.*

Psalm 100:4

There's a certain etiquette that is appropriate for deer hunters to follow when using property that belongs to a resident owner. If we go on the land in the waking hours, it is best to not go directly to the deerstand. Instead, it is a courtesy to take the time to stop and greet the owner if he or she is at home and available for a brief visit. This allows you the opportunity to offer a word of thanks for the privilege to hunt and alert the owner to your specific whereabouts, which will ensure his good graces.

How rude it would be to always go through the gates of the farm, blast by the landowner with a hurried wave, and go straight to the "goodies" the property offers. It would be akin to a dinner guest knocking on your door and, after you open it, ignore you, brush by you, and go directly to your table. There he proceeds to help himself to your hard-earned, carefully prepared food. Wouldn't you feel unappreciated? Sure you would.

There's a picture in this for those of us who go to the Lord in prayer. So many times we open up with, "Our Father in heaven." Those words are the knock at His door. If our very next words include statements such as, "do this" or "do that," then for all intents and purposes we have walked by the Master of the house and, as someone once quipped, "gone straight to His pantry."

On the other hand, to follow our opener with the courtesies noted in today's verse means we have properly come into His presence.

"Enter His gates with thanksgiving." That alone could keep us at God's door for the rest of our days. Because He has granted us untold blessings for which to be grateful, to try to express them all each time we pray would be impossible. Instead, we can take a few moments to list several of His blessings that are currently on our hearts.

One of the instances when I can be guilty of improper entry into God's presence is at the supper table. It is such a brief visit and more often than not the prayer is handled with less than the best of care. Too many times it sounds like, "Dear Lord, bless this food we are about to receive. Amen!" With very little effort and extra time the prayer could be improved: "Dear Lord, thank You for Your abundant provision. You are our kind God, and we appreciate Your care for us." With something similar to that as the opener, I have then followed the example of "entering His gates with thanksgiving."

The second phase is to "enter His courts with praise." In the same way a hunter compliments a farmer for his kindness and the beauty of his property, one who goes to the Lord can applaud His attributes. Honoring His majesty, glory, omnipotence, and any other divine qualities that our hearts are aware of reveals our respectful hearts.

There are always exceptions to the rules, of course. There will be situations, such as (gulp!) falling out of a treestand, when we must cry out for help and mercy. In that moment, our hearts instantly recognize God's great abilities and His kind willingness to deliver us. Going to Him first is in itself a high compliment to His power. But to always pray in this way is something we should work to change.

By remembering to make the effort to not go directly to the deerstand on someone else's property, we can be reminded to not go to God's house and make the discourteous mistake of going straight to His pantry!

O Lord, I know I need to enter into Your holy presence in the proper manner. Thank You for Your kindness and patience in giving me an example to follow. "Our Father who is in heaven, hallowed be Your name. Your kingdom come. Your will be done, on earth as it is in heaven. Give us this day our daily bread. And forgive us our debts, as we also have forgiven our debtors. And do not lead us into temptation, but deliver us from evil. For Yours is the kingdom and the power and the glory forever." Amen.

38

He Can, Can He?

All things are possible to him who believes.

Mark 9:23

A funny thing happens in my head when a buck is coming toward my stand. If the deer's approach is slow, giving me time to mull over the shot, my mind bounces back and forth, sounding as if I'm talking about another person: "Can he make the shot?" "He can." "Can he?" One reveals confidence; the other shows doubt.

I would almost rather a deer surprise me with a sudden appearance so I can react with the skills I have developed. But more often than not, I end up in the mental tug of war between *can* and *can't*. Fortunately, *can* has won the skirmish most times.

This struggle between "he can" and "can he?" has a familiar ring. In the Gospels of Matthew and Mark, two perceptions of Christ are recorded. They represent an incredibly important application. In Matthew 8:2 it is said, "And a leper came to Him and bowed down before Him, and said, 'Lord, if You are willing, You can make me clean.'" The terminally ill man didn't indicate any doubt in Christ's ability to heal. He only asked if Jesus was willing. The result was a cleansing from his leprosy.

The opposite attitude is found in Mark 9:22. A father had brought his demon-possessed son to Jesus. Since childhood the boy had torturous episodes of convulsing, falling to the ground, and rolling about while foaming at the mouth. Sadly, the father revealed a heart lacking belief when he said, "If You can do anything, take pity on us and help us!"

Jesus must have noticed the word *if*. His response was an indictment of the father's shortness of faith. I imagine it might have been with raised eyebrows that Christ showed His surprise, and said, "'If You can?' All things are possible to him who believes." Feeling the sting of the tone of Jesus' words, the desperate father immediately had a change of heart and cried, "I do believe; help my unbelief." His son received deliverance.

Although the outcome was glorious in both cases, the father of the demon-possessed son had much to learn from his lack of faith. Like him, our own faith seems to falter at times. It is an awesome moment when doubt gives way to confidence in Christ's ability to perform the miraculous. This flip-flop that takes us from defeat to victory is a work of the Holy Spirit in our lives. It happens when we suddenly realize whom we are addressing.

The next time a bruiser buck makes your brain swing between confidence and doubt, may it remind you of a struggle and response that reaches beyond a trophy kill: "All things are possible to him who believes."

Blessed Father, thank You for Your patience when I stumble. May Your Holy Spirit continue to remind me of who I am addressing when I come to You with my needs. Draw me close, Father, and forgive me for my lack of faith. In Jesus' name, amen.

39

Thanks, Adam!

Then to Adam He said, "Because you have listened to the voice of your wife, and have eaten from the tree about which I commanded you, saying 'You shall not eat from it'; cursed is the ground because of you....Both thorns and thistles it shall grow for you."

Genesis 3:17,18

People tell me I'm a reasonably patient fellow who is generally not too quick to fly off the handle. They say it takes quite a lot to rattle me. These kind folks, however, have yet to be near me when I'm in a brier thicket tracking an arrowed deer. They haven't observed me when every step is being thwarted by relentless, spiny claws. I can't stand them!

As the thousands of tiny spears that line the tangled branches tear at my clothes and turn them into shredded cotton, I quickly change from a mild-mannered soul to a tooth-grinding grumbler. And the vocalization of my anger is not usually subdued—it is audible and delivered with abandon. When the briers rip at my costly camo and my flesh, it is tempting to use some "colorful" words. I am aware of the need to maintain a certain level of integrity, so I make a concerted effort to limit my verbiage to a form of righteous indignation. It's not an easy task, but I do my best.

Of all the things I can say about the thorns that fight my every move, there are two words, when spoken out loud, that seem to be good therapy for my rage. These noncurse words usually come when I have to repeatedly remove my hat and gloves off branches that have grabbed them. They are: *"Thanks, Adam!"*

When I resort to this phrase, I am not casting blame. I am simply recognizing that the mess I am trying to plow through is literally a product of the original sin of Adam. When he disobeyed God and the ground was cursed, little did he know that his choice would be felt by a lone hunter far into the future—outside the Garden, across the great waters, in a land called America, in a state called Tennessee. And Adam couldn't have known that his name would fall so resentfully from that hunter's lips. But far worse than this, Adam didn't know that the day would come when thorns, one of earth's most annoying evidences of mankind's sin of transgression, would be cruelly used in mockery to crown the innocent one as He died on the cross. (Remember this the next time the thorns draw your blood!)

If there is one thing good that a battle with a brier patch can yield, it is the reminder that I have two children who may someday have children, who in turn may bear offspring. In the same way that Adam's choice to sin affected my life (in more ways than just torn camo), what I do today could cause others in the future to experience unneeded entanglements. May their future never find them stuck woefully in the middle of emotional or spiritual thorns as a result of my disobedience. And may it never come to pass that any of them would angrily say, "Thanks, Dad!" or "Thanks, Grandpa!" The thought that my name would ever be uttered with the slightest tone of disgust is too sad to ponder. That very idea motivates me to live righteously.

None of us is going to be a perfect ancestor. Through careful obedience and a daily pursuit of Christlikeness, we can avoid being dishonored in the years ahead by unwise decisions made today.

Allow God to clear the ugly brier bushes in your heart because, someday, others will be dealing with the path you followed.

Dear Lord, thank You for listening to my heart today. Your mighty hand to deliver me from being a source of thorns in another person's life is something I need. Clear away the unholy growth in the soil of my flesh. I trust You to make the ground of time passable for those who come behind me. In Jesus' name I humbly ask this, amen.

40

Bottle and Book

*You have taken account of my wanderings; put my tears in
Your bottle. Are they not in Your book?*

Psalm 56:8

Two of the most important items in my day pack that
goes with me to the deerstand are my water bottle and my
little book of Scriptures. Both items meet a specific thirst.
The water is especially important if I make a shot and
have to spend significant time and serious energy
tracking an animal. This is especially crucial in the early,
warmer parts of the archery season here in Tennessee.

The Bible is a blessing to a thirsty soul. The contents
quench the need to not let a day pass without hearing
from the God who loves both our bodies and souls. The
thirst in my spirit is something the flesh often fights.
Though it tries to keep me from drinking from the
Bible's pages, I know to ignore God's Word will leave me
dry in my heart.

As I was in the woods taking in God's Word one day,
I saw something interesting in light of what I carry in my
day pack. God, too, has a bottle and a book. Today's verse
references this and tells us He stores something very special in those items. They don't contain a source for His
longings or something to satisfy a need. Instead, they
hold the record of those times we desperately thirsted for
Him. Our tears of affliction are kept in His divine con-

tainer as well as on the stained pages of the journal He keeps of our lives.

God has preserved the tears of Job, the countless captives, the oppressed, Jeremiah, and the widow of Nain (see Job 16:20; Psalm 126:5; Ecclesiastes 4:1; Jeremiah 9:1; Luke 7:11-15). It's amazing to think that in that same bottle and on those pages are the tears of my own father and mother when they said farewell to their dying parents and family members. Also stored in that container are my wife's tears she shed during the painful delivery of our children. And there, too, are the precious tears that fell from the tender cheeks of my kids when they realized they needed a Savior. God cares for us so much that He has not forgotten one salty drop that has ever fallen—or will ever fall—from our eyes. All our deepest groanings are kept in His care.

If you have a water bottle or a Bible with you in your pack, take them out and look at them, drink from both and remember God's great love for you!

Oh merciful and loving Father, thank You for the care You have given to my tears. I am humbled to know You have held on to them all this time. You alone are able to comfort me and cause me to forget the pain they represent. Blessed be Your name for this display of how much You love me. In Jesus, Your holy Son's name, amen.

41

The Condo

Beware that you do not forget the LORD your God.

Deuteronomy 8:11

I sat beside my son, Nathan, in a treestand we affection-
ately called "The Condo." It wore that name because
there was plenty of room in it for both of us. Our friend
had built it with good sturdy lumber, and it featured a
bench with a comfortable backrest. There was only one
flaw. Due to the way one of the tree's limbs had grown,
there was an open spot in the floor. To bypass the
problem all we had to do when we climbed in was step
around it. One of us had to straddle it with his feet when
we were sitting. Nathan ended up at that spot.

The morning was quiet as we monitored the large
field. There was no talking, just watching. After about 30
minutes I slowly turned my head to look at my son. His
eyes were drooping and his head was beginning to bob. I
could tell that the drool of dozing was only seconds away.
When his shoulders slumped he leaned forward a little.
Suddenly, out of nowhere, he let out a scream that seemed
to shake the entire farm. After a moment's recovery he
started to laugh. I controlled my disappointment that our
hunt was probably over and asked him what had happened.

"Oh, Dad!" he stated with a noticeable shortness of breath. "I fell into a deep sleep. When I woke up and opened my eyes I was looking down. All I saw was the ground through the opening in the floor. I just knew I was falling out of the sky!" Thus the bloodcurdling scream. Then we both had a good laugh that continues to this day each time we remember the incident.

Some hunters who have tumbled out of treestands after falling asleep in them might agree that too much comfort up there can be dangerous. The Condo is proof. It might have been better if there were some strategically placed nails in the seat or in the backrest to lightly dig at our flesh and keep us alert. Instead, it was cozy to a fault.

The hazard that excessive ease creates is not limited to treestands. For those of us who belong to God and who live in a nation that is blessed with so much wealth at our fingertips, a very real pitfall awaits. Allowing ourselves to become overly comfortable and knowingly relaxed in our abundant possessions is a dangerous state of heart. It can lead us to the tragedy of pridefully forgetting our need for God. The wandering Israelites in Moses' day proved this to be true over and over again. They watched God richly supply their every need, then they turned away from Him when their bellies were full. It's a sad commentary on one of the greatest weaknesses of mankind.

I could have spared Nathan his treestand trauma if I had elbowed him when I saw him beginning to drift into sleep. That would have salvaged the hunt. As for our potential to be too much at ease with our lives and disregard our dependency on our heavenly Father, the Holy Spirit wants us to heed His nudges now. He wants to deliver us in advance from the results of our complacency and help us be on the alert at all times. Take note of Moses' words of warning in Deuteronomy 8:11-14:

> Beware that you do not forget the Lord your God by not keeping His commandments.... Otherwise, when you have eaten and are satisfied, and have built good houses...and your silver and gold multiply, and all that you have multiplies, then your heart will become proud and you will forget the LORD your God who brought you out from the land of Egypt, out of the house of slavery.

To not respond to this divine elbow in our fleshly sides will result in a very real fall! Take the time today to remember who alone has abundantly supplied your needs.

Father, thank You for Your bountiful provision. I confess that all I have, will have, or ever hope to have is from Your mighty and loving hands. Help me never forget You in times of abundance and remember to thank You for the gift of need. It reminds me that I am hopeless without You. Help my deepest longing to be for You and not what You give. Blessed be Your name, amen.

42

Middle Seat

He saw a large crowd,
and felt compassion for them.
Matthew 14:14

Rarely had I longed for the solitude of a deerstand as much as the day Annie and I boarded a flight to Dallas. The overbooked plane exiled us to middle seats in separate rows surrounded by strangers. As I sat there, squeezed by my extra-large male neighbors, it wasn't long before I realized the fellow next to the window had some type of serious respiratory condition. His cough was preceded by a deep draw of air that was accompanied by a distinct and disturbing wheeze. The instant his lungs were at full capacity, he would begin his cough. It was one loud and continuous gurgling sound followed by several short, thrashing finishes. I was sure something had broken loose in his body the first time I heard it.

I cringed and tried to roll up into an impenetrable ball, hoping to repel any of the deadly germs that might escape the man's innards. It was a sickening experience. Fearing that he may have been a victim of some terminal form of cancer or other disease, I didn't say anything. I didn't want to risk offending him.

As if he weren't enough to deal with, an irritating problem started behind me. The amazing little girl was about five years old. She was using her seat-back tray to do her daily quota of handstands, and I was taking a beating. I kept waiting for her parents to correct her behavior, but they didn't. Along with the tiny pest behind me, across the aisle and two rows up were a couple of people who were talking loudly enough to compete with the volume of the jet engines. It might have been fine if their conversation had been interesting. Unfortunately, their loud prattle was boring and, at times, very lewd.

Needless to say, I was not a happy flyer. I knew the next two hours were going to be comparable to a root canal. I began to detest the bodies around me as well as everyone else on board. Though we were all divided by aisles and armrests, the crowd seemed to be closing in on me. I had no place to run.

Then, without warning, right in the middle of another lung-whipping cough next to me, a question came to my mind that made me uncomfortable: "If Jesus were sitting in this seat, how would He handle this situation?"

I felt embarrassed. My less-than-friendly feelings about those around me were generated by my complete lack of care for them. I didn't like the cougher, the kid, or the conversationalists. I had no affection for them, only rejection. I knew that Jesus' reaction, on the other hand, would have been quite different: "He saw a large crowd, and felt compassion for them."

The Savior would have likely healed the man sitting next to me, invited the child to come up and sit on His lap, and reasoned some sense into the talkers nearby. For Him, the flight would have been much too short, lacking the time to touch each one where he or she sat.

I was moved that day as I pondered my pitiful attitude in light of the Lord's love for people. I determined to do something about it. Before the plane landed in Dallas, I had managed to make a new friend. It was not the coughing machine next to me; he had finally gone to sleep (not dead, just asleep!). Instead, I discovered the other fellow was a delightful, young, first-time flyer who needed the comforting confidence of a veteran air traveler.

As I later reflected on my change of heart, I realized that while I was giving of myself to my row partner, I couldn't hear the sounds that had irritated me earlier. It's a phenomenon that seems to always occur when I look away from myself and see the needs of my neighbors. Being moved by compassion is as much a blessing to the one who extends it as it is to the one who receives it. Such is the way of Christ. Having His attitude of benevolence makes a long journey sweeter.

Thank You, Lord, for Your abundant compassion that You have shown me. You are worthy of my praise because You alone are good. Help me to see other people's needs as more important than my own. I know if I do, it will redeem the time You give to me here on earth. In Your kind and holy name I pray, amen.

43

Guilty Till
Proven Innocent

When you were dead in your transgressions...
He made you alive together with Him...having canceled
out the certificate of debt consisting of decrees against us,
which was hostile to us; and He has taken it out of the way,
having nailed it to the cross.

Colossians 2:13,14

There is a rule of law in our land that is humanly fair and equitable for all who have allegedly committed crimes. Though they may be guilty of the deed, the law demands that they are "innocent until proven guilty." While this may be the rule in the courts, it is not one I carry into the woods when I go deer hunting.

Years ago, when I first began to pursue the wary whitetail, I learned very quickly that a sound I thought was merely the dainty scampering of a chipmunk or a squirrel was really a deer moving through the brush. Too many times I made the erroneous assumption that the sound was one critter's noise, when in fact it was that of another. After several misreads, I finally decided to consider every sound as suspect. I adopted that attitude and maintain it to this day. When I hear the slightest crunch in the leaves and can't identify the source by sight, I immediately think "guilty till proven innocent!" This method has yielded good results, and I have plenty of empty rifle shells and bloody, broken arrows to prove it.

There was a time in my life when, like an elusive buck trying to sneak past a hunter, I attempted to slip by God. It was my intent to get around His all-seeing eye and, without accountability to Him, enjoy the unholy pleasures of this world. I had no affection for God's ways, only contempt for His truth. In my heart of flesh there was nothing good. Like David confessed in Psalm 51:5: "Behold, I was brought forth in iniquity, and in sin my mother conceived me." My very thoughts were opposed to God's holiness. I was "by nature a child of wrath" (see Ephesians 2:3). Because I was born with a propensity to sin, I was doomed to be the target of the flaming arrows of God's judgment.

Thankfully, however, the Father of all things heard me and saw me and knew I was "guilty until proven innocent." I was *guilty* of having a sinful nature and needed desperately to be *made innocent*. And, in the way that a passing whitetail could never make something different of itself, God knew I could in no way exonerate myself. It was then that the miracle of miracles happened! Colossians 1:21,22 describes it: "And although you were formerly alienated and hostile in mind, engaged in evil deeds, yet He has now reconciled you in His fleshly body through death, in order to present you before Him holy and blameless and beyond reproach." Thanks be to God that He saved me from the eternal consequences of my sinful nature! By accepting Christ I was transformed from impending death to eternal life. How great is His grace!

If you have allowed God to make you acceptable in His sight through Christ, rejoice! And, if you hear a sound that suddenly arouses your hunter's suspicion, let it remind you that God once heard you and found you.

Heavenly Father, thank You for canceling the certificate of debt that would have found me guilty. By nailing it to the cross of Your Son, Jesus, I have been made acceptable in Your sight. Without that kind of love for me, I would surely have been sentenced to eternal destruction. Blessed be Your name and the name of Jesus, the blameless one. Forever and ever, amen.

44

Scoot Over

So show your love for the alien.
Deuteronomy 10:19

There is a farm I hunt near my home in Tennessee. It's a 15-mile drive on a rural highway lined with fields of tobacco crops. When spring arrives, they fill up with migrant workers, mostly from Mexico. The hundreds of individuals can be seen laboring tirelessly from planting time in May until harvest is completed near November. The population of the foreigners grows in number each year.

Many of the farmers who hire them and oversee their coming are very positive about their presence. One man told me he could not be happier with the work ethic he found in his laborers. Their willingness to work overshadowed their inability to communicate efficiently in English. He paid them a very good wage and said he looks forward to the new growing season so he can see the friends he has made over the past few years.

While the migrant laborers may be welcomed by some, others have developed a contempt for the "different" workers. Some interesting conversations and quips can be heard at our local establishments. My ears have been privy to some less-than-kind remarks about those who bear little resemblance to the rest of us.

Each time I hear a derogatory statement about the foreigners in our land, I can't help but think of the command given to the Israelites through Moses in Deuteronomy 10:18,19: "He executes justice for the orphan and the widow, and shows His love for the alien by giving him food and clothing. So show your love for the alien, for you were aliens in the land of Egypt." The "outsiders" were tenderly linked with the orphan and the widow. This indicates the affection God must have for those who are displaced.

There is a truth that is overlooked by far too many people in our country. The immigrants that are visible to us, though temporary, are ultimately a gauge for the quality of our faith in Christ. If we treat them unkindly we are ignoring our former status as spiritual aliens. Consider these selected portions of Scripture:

> Remember that formerly you, the Gentiles in the flesh...were at that time separate from Christ, excluded from the commonwealth of Israel, and strangers to the covenants of promise, having no hope and without God in the world. But now in Christ Jesus you who formerly were far off have been brought near by the blood of Christ. For He Himself is our peace, who made both groups into one and broke down the barrier of the dividing wall, by abolishing in His flesh the enmity (Ephesians 2:11-15).

> Through Him we both have our access in one Spirit to the Father. So then you are no longer strangers and aliens, but you are fellow citizens with the saints, and are of God's household (verses 18,19).

What causes us to go from remembering to forgetting our former rank as aliens to Christ? And why would we mistreat the strangers among us? Perhaps it is the excessive comfort we have come to know and are not so willing to share. Or it may be a fear that "they" will become a permanent fixture in our landscape. For whatever reason, we withhold our kindness to foreigners, and this is a wrong and dangerous attitude. By not showing love for the alien we run the risk of gaining the displeasure of the one who has clothed and fed us by His love. The effects of His wrath are far greater than the small effort it takes to "scoot over" and let the newcomers have some room.

Since you are a hunter and your passion for the great outdoors takes you into the rural regions of America, you too may be seeing more foreigners these days. Or maybe a growing number of aliens have moved in to your town. Wherever you are, if your good attitude toward foreign workers is being challenged, use it to help you never forget that at one time God was kind to you when you were lost, and He welcomed you into His family.

Oh God, thank You for the love You have shown to every person through Your Son. Help me never forget how You made me a part of Your household even though I was a stranger. I pray for grace to extend Your love to others who have come to this country. Forgive me for the times I have failed in this regard. In Jesus' name, amen.

45

Seize the Moment

Sanctify Christ as Lord in your hearts,
always being ready to make a defense to everyone who
asks you to give an account for the hope
that is in you, yet with gentleness and reverence.

1 Peter 3:15

I have seen and heard some interesting ways that folks have made known the sobering truth that someday all of us will meet our Maker. One of my favorite examples took place in Knoxville, Tennessee. A farmer owned some land at one end of a regional commercial airport. Though personally I never saw it, I was told that on a hillside, for all passengers and crew to see as they departed the runway, the farmer had constructed a message. I'm not sure what material he used, but the words were, "PREPARE TO MEET THY GOD!"

I have a feeling the cleverly placed warning found its way into many a heart, especially if there was turbulence on takeoff or a sudden, unusual mechanical noise. The nervous souls were probably quite moved by the truth in the farmer's message. I'm not sure if the guy's sermon on his mount is still there, but I have no doubt that it remains in the minds and hearts of those who saw it.

Another timely delivery of the "get ready" message was made by my son, Nathan. He was 15 years old when he and I were walking down our sidewalk on the way to our van. Annie and our daughter, Heidi, were already aboard, along with some precious friends who were visiting. It was Sunday morning, and we were going to church. For some strange reason I asked, "Son, would you like to drive us?" His learner's permit was a just a few weeks old, and I honestly don't know what possessed me to put our guests in such danger. Before I could recant, Nathan excitedly responded, "Oh, Dad, I'd love to!"

I gave him the keys and he climbed into the driver's seat. I got in through the side door, smiled at our company, sat down in my seat, and put on my helmet. (Okay, the helmet part is not true.) Nathan started the engine and, as I had taught him, let it warm up before driving away. During the brief wait he decided to do a little evangelism. He turned in his chair and looked back through the van. Everyone knew he was a novice driver, and there was a certain tension in the air. With a sheepish grin, he asked, "Is everyone…" He paused just long enough for all of his passengers to look his way, then finished the question with a loud, "…saved?"

I'm sure his well-timed inquiry was as much for me as anyone else. He knew how unsettled I was by allowing him to drive, so he seized the moment. That boy is sharp! We all got a good laugh, then secretly tightened our safety belts when Nathan turned to face the front. (Obviously, we survived the day.)

Taking advantage of opportunity is a key to effective evangelism. As we go about our daily lives, whether on the job, in a crowd, or in the woods with friends, let's make the moments count by spreading the word about our eventual meeting with God. The fact is undeniable: "It is appointed for men to die once and after this comes judgment" (Hebrews 9:27). What hope can we offer to those who hear our message and are filled with terror? John 3:16: "For God so loved the world, that He gave His only begotten Son, that whoever believes in Him shall not perish, but have eternal life."

Someone offered this sobering advice: "Tell them that Jesus died for them. It will cost you nothing to say it, but it will cost them everything not to know!" How true.

Father in heaven, thank You for Your provision of salvation through Your blessed Son, Jesus. Thank You that someone took the time to tell me that You alone can save. Help me recognize opportunities to share this good news with others and have the boldness to seize the moment. Until You come I pray in Jesus' name, amen.

About the Author

Proudly claiming West Virginia as his home state, Steve Chapman grew up as the son of a preacher. He met his wife, Annie, in junior high school in 1963. In March of 1975, they married after dating a few months and settled in Nashville, Tennessee. There they have raised their son and daughter, Nathan and Heidi.

Steve is president of S&A Family, Inc., an organization formed to oversee the production of the Chapman's recorded music. They have had "family life" as the theme of their lyrics since they began singing together in 1980. As Dove Award-winning artists, their schedule sends them to over 100 cities a year to present concerts that feature songs from over 15 recorded projects.

Steve's love of hunting began in his early teens on a weekend when one of his dad's church members invited him to tag along on an October squirrel hunt. Archery is his first choice for use in the field, followed by muzzle loader, and then pistol or rifle. To date, according to Steve's calculations, he has entered the woods before daylight on at least a thousand mornings. He says he hopes for just as many more.

As a member of API's pro-staff team, Steve uses and endorses API treestands.

Reel Time with God

by Steve Chapman

Perfectly sized for keeping in a tackle box or backpack, *Reel Time with God* shares the delights of standing next to streams, lakes, and saltwater with a rod and reel while gently reminding fishermen that God is the true source of life...and fish!

While reveling in the wide variety of fish and methods of catching them, outdoorsman Steve Chapman casts into the deep pools of God's Word and lands spiritual truths that will inspire readers to seek a deeper relationship with God and reflect godly values in their homes, careers, and relationships. Highlighting the thrills of hooking big ones, these vibrant stories and reflections joyfully honor God for His love and provision.
